Diana Burgwyn · Salzburg: a portrait

Diana Burgwyn

Salzburg
a portrait

Alfred Winter
Edition

For Jim and Ivy,

*my beloved companions
in the Salzburg adventure*

CONTENTS

FOREWORD

Just as a portrait in oils seeks, with the strokes of a brush, to reveal the inner vitality of a person, so this book attempts to do with the city of Salzburg through the medium of words.

Because it was written by a foreigner, it depicts Salzburg somewhat differently from the work of a native. And, because it is a portrait, it emphasizes certain aspects of its subject's personality at the expense of others.

Salzburg is an old city but not a museum. It is vibrant with life. That life is best understood in the context of history. Hence this book stresses the links between past and present and tries occasionally to look into the future.

It is the author's hope that English-speaking visitors, particularly Americans, will find SALZBURG: A PORTRAIT geared to their special interests. If the book succeeds in portraying Salzburg to these readers as the fascinating and unique city that it truly is, rather than merely as the setting for isolated curiosities – summer festival, baroque architecture, Alpine views – then it will have achieved its purpose.

Diana Stambul Burgwyn

PRELUDE. SALZBURG THE ENCHANTRESS

The city of Salzburg has won a great number of admirers during its long life. Among these, many have been ardently vocal about their feelings.

There was, for instance, German master singer Hans Sachs who came to Salzburg in 1549 and was so impressed with both locale and cuisine that he produced a song about it all. Composer Franz Schubert several centuries later wrote to his brother from Salzburg that its valley was "as beautiful as Elysium or Paradise."

For those inclined to statistics, mention should be made of Alexander von Humboldt, scientist and traveler who, back in 1798, proclaimed Salzburg to be one of the three loveliest cities in the world, the others being Naples and Constantinople. (Admittedly, that verbal bouquet has not been appreciated by some Salzburgers whose devotion to their city is such that they cannot bear its glory being shared.)

The list of Salzburg devotées is as diverse as it is long. Author James Joyce, England's King Edward VIII, suffragette Jane Addams, maestro Arturo Toscanini and the sultry Marlene Dietrich succumbed to its magic, as do present-day American presidents who partake of high-level talks amidst the Alpine splendor. Even certain sea gulls, whose native habitat is east Prussia, have the sensible habit of wintering here along the grey-green river Salzach.

One of the few persons of note who did *not* fall for Salzburg was its native son Wolfgang Amadeus Mozart. He has his reasons – but more on Mozart later. The fact is, Salzburg has stood well the test of time, its beauty as striking to modern eyes as to those of centuries past. More arguable is the question of what makes it so beautiful.

Opinions aside for a moment, let's consider some facts. The city is capital of the state or province (in German, the word is *Land*) of the same name; there are eight other such divisions in Austria. Though only 29 square miles in area, Salzburg has 145,000 inhabitants, making this the nation's fourth most populous city. Added to that a whopping number of tourists – some 670,000 annually – who flock here to enjoy the music, architecture, cuisine, handmade crafts, spas, convention facilities and nearby ski slopes and lakes. They fill the elegant old hotels, the tall new ones, the converted castles, hilltop chalets and the spotless private homes whose *Zimmer frei* ("rooms vacant") signs dot the landscape.

Salzburg is located in the heart of Europe near Austria's western border with Germany; it lies at the transition between the high ranges of the Alps and the flat country surrounding them. Because of its proximity to German Bavaria (whose capital is Munich) and to Austria's own Tyrol (capital, Innsbruck), outsiders tend to consider Salzburg as part of one or the other region, but it is separate in both geography and sentiment.

Salzburg is situated on both banks of the river Salzach ("Salt River"), enjoying the natural protection of three hills: the Kapuzinerberg ("Capuchin Mountain") on the north or right bank and the Mönchsberg ("Monk's Mountain") and Festungsberg ("Fortress Mountain") on the south or left bank. Ranges of other, loftier mountains surround the city, green in summer, ermine-cloaked in winter. The so-called Old City lies on the left bank of the Salzach, clustered at the foot of the Mönchsberg and in the shadow of the medieval fortress Hohensalzburg ("High Salzburg"), the city's proudest landmark. The new part of the city, which isn't new at all – a settlement called "Am Stein" existed there in the ninth century – lies on the right bank; one can walk for miles on this side. The Staatsbrücke ("State Bridge"), one of several not very attractive structures connecting the two parts, can be considered the center of Salzburg.

In centuries past the gently curving Salzach was an important commercial river, busy with shipping of salt, primarily, as well as peat, copper, silver, gold and other commodities. It was also a source of fear for residents, since constant flooding brought disastrous consequences to human life and habitation. Only since the mid 19th century has the river been restrained and regulated by high embankment walls. On planning the taming of their exuberant stream, the city fathers at first had intended to direct the waters through an absolutely straight canal; however, a local painter, opposed to tampering with the Salzach's God-given contours, fought this. He had to form a political party to win his point – but win he did.

Modern Salzburg has its origins almost 1300 years ago against the rocky walls of the Mönchsberg where St. Peter's, the first monastic settlement, was founded. It being customary then for spiritual domains to remain separate from areas populated by secular dependents and employees, there arose nearer to the river a medieval burghers' quarter, with crooked, narrow streets and three- and four-storey houses set closely together (even then Salzburg had

10

limited space, so buildings were planned high rather than wide). Most of these wooden homes were destroyed in a series of fires, but you can still find an occasional one as well as many examples of similar 15th–19th century structures, the later ones being of stone. Largely devoid of ornamentation, one much like the others externally, such dwellings achieved what little individuality they had in the lovely interior courtyards; these afforded sunlight lacking in the houses themselves.

In the early Middle Ages the heart of the burghers' (or commoners') town was Waagplatz which served as market and meeting place and housed the courts of justice; a tavern was built for merriment and a gallows for more somber purposes. Even the big scales for weighing were located here; hence the name Waagplatz ("Weighing Square"). As the city expanded westward the market moved to the present Alter Markt ("Old Market Place") and the most important thoroughfare became Getreidegasse, which historians now tell us means "Busy Street" (not "Grain Street" as they used to think); this thoroughfare runs right up to the rocky edge of the Mönchsberg. Getreidegasse boasts Mozart's birthplace, now a museum, and is full of shops whose intricate wrought iron signs are justifiably renowned.* Also notable here are examples of Salzburg's characteristic *Grabendächer* ("trough roofs" or "ditch roofs"). These have long fascinated painters, 19th century Rudolf Alt among them, because the houses featuring them appear to be roofless. In fact, rooves do exist, being broken into a series of peaked gables hidden from the street by high rectangular house fronts which give the impression of another storey.

Walking along these and other streets of the Old City, one comes upon many other hints of life in past centuries. Often the names provide clues: Klampferergasse ("Tinsmith's Lane"); Brodgasse ("Bread Street") where the old bread market stood; Judengasse ("Jews Street"), a segregated quarter for Salzburg's Jewish residents; even a Krotachgasse ("Toad Street") named after the toads found in pools there.

---

* Those interested in wrought iron should not miss the beautiful Renaissance screen surrounding the Florian Fountain on the Alter Markt.

Moving to the right bank of the city, part of which was destroyed during a terrible fire in 1818, the main artery is Linzer Gasse, so named because this used to be the old post road to Linz (and also Wels); both ends could be closed by gates. This and many other of the wonderful old city gates, decorative as well as effective defense measures, were pulled down for reasons of traffic. Imbergstrasse, shaded by fine chestnut trees, is notable for its stately old homes. From ancient Steingasse ("Stone Street") wagons full of merchandise left for Italy during the Middle Ages; the homes on this street were not infrequently damaged by flooding of the Salzach, accompanied by powerful, brackish river smells. Once again the names reveal trades carried out in the various streets: Lederergasse ("Leather Street") is one, and Königsgässchen ("Little Street of the King") another. The latter is named after the "night king" whose unsavory job it was to empty the cesspools at night.

As Salzburg grew from a monastic settlement into an ever more important ecclesiastical principality with a ruling archbishop – we shall meet several of these worldly and often earthy gentlemen later – the separation between the commoners and their princely leaders was carried out architecturally with increasing form and order. The most imaginative planning took place during the late 16th century rule of Archbishop Wolf Dietrich who ruthlessly tore down public buildings and residents' homes in the Old City in order to create a number of magnificent squares bedecked with fountains and statuary. These squares were to serve as a backdrop for great buildings, among them the Cathedral and the official home of the archbishops, the Residenz.

Small and compact, Salzburg lends itself both to planned excursions with specific sites in mind and to adventures with no route but where the senses lead: the aromas of smoked meats, lavender, woodruff, the sound of church bells – each voice clearly identifiable to the discerning listener, the glimpse of a dark, narrow *Durchgang;* these characteristic "arcades" lead through house fronts to another street or sometimes to a sunny square with splashing fountain. (In winter Salzburg's many fountains are encased and padlocked in wooden shelters to protect them from the elements.)

Salzburg was once a walled city, almost impregnable to attack and with sturdy bastions on all sides. One can see remnants of these fortifications as well as the few remaining city gates (the Gstötten, Klausen and Stein). Many other hints of the past are tantalizing: a romanesque stone lion in Sigmund-Haffner-Gasse, a 16th century pharmacy on the Alter Markt, memorial tablets in marble everywhere (here composer Hugo Wolf stayed, there geographer Alexander von Humboldt, in this house German socialist August Bebel worked, in that one scientist Paracelsus mixed his potions). Also numerous are the ruling archbishop's coats-of-arms, the *Wappen*. Signatures in marble, they appear on edifices around the town, telling us who built what; Leonhard von Keutschach's symbol was a beetroot, Markus Sittikus' a capering mountain goat, Paris Lodron's a lion with knotted tail.

Once one has perused the city and determined one's favorites from among the passages and squares, the castles and churches,* there are the many charming suburbs, like Mülln, Aigen, Morzg, Anif, Maria Plain; these can be easily reached by bus. Incidentally, the public transportation system in Salzburg is a good one. For those who do not wish to give in to modern means of transit but are a bit foot-weary, the town still has its oldtime horse and buggy creations known as *Fiaker,* which line up along the Residenzplatz awaiting customers. The horses are clothed in plaid blankets, their noses buried in feed bags while the drivers, sporting Tyrolean hats, snooze between trips. Well versed in local lore, the drivers make up in color for what they sometimes lack in accuracy.

Returning to that elusive subject of Salzburg's beauty, most authorities agree that a key ingredient is the harmony between the man-made city and its glorious natural surroundings – one inseparable from the other. That man was able so perfectly to adapt his creations to nature's in a constricted area and with such a remarkable sense of proportion was a stunning achievement. Perhaps this fusion was most poetically described by Hermann Bahr who wrote that Salzburg is "nature become spirit, spirit turned to stone."

Bahr was a Linz-born poet and literary and social critic who also worked as theater director under Max Reinhardt, co-founder of the Salzburg Festival. Having lived here from 1912 to 1922, he was constantly absorbing and analyzing the city's enchantment. For him and many others, Salzburg is architecturally and spiritually a child of Italy, "the German Rome." Bahr felt the city's integrated wholeness to be an Italian characteristic (he likened Salzburg to an opera set to music in all details). He saw a second parallel with Italy in that the homes of inhabitants are not particularly striking; one's attention is riveted immediately on churches, monasteries, castles – the official buildings.

* See chapters 4 and 5.

13

As we shall see in uncovering the layers of Salzburg's history, the city was unquestionably and continually influenced by Italy. Indeed, the same Wolf Dietrich to whom Salzburg owes its central squares was himself related to the Medicis and was passionately drawn to the Renaissance magnificence of Rome. There are, however, those who feel the Italian connection is pressed too far. One of them is a present-day art historian whose name, somewhat confusingly, is Hermann Bauer. To describe Salzburg as an Italian city, says Bauer, is to misunderstand it completely, though he agrees it was modeled on Italian lines. That it has no monumental buildings of colossal proportions is for him one among many distinctly non-Italian features. Rather, Salzburg is "a gateway to the south".

Bauer challenges, too, the common reference to Salzburg as a baroque city. True, many of its buildings date from the 16th to 18th century and the city's single greatest architect, Fischer von Erlach, was of that period, but the calculated town planning is, Bauer insists, rather a Renaissance characteristic as are the clusters of burghers' homes whose arcades and underpasses combine intimacy with accessibility.

To be sure, however one defines Salzburg's predominant architectural motif, there is no question that the fusion of diverse styles was masterly. One need only consider a single building, the Franziskanerkirche ("Franciscan Church") which combines the romanesque, gothic and baroque, to realize this.

And so it goes – the analysis of the beauty which is so concrete, yet spiritual; so real, yet virtually impossible to transmit fully in words. Individuals who write about Salzburg disagree on another point: from which of its several peaks (Bauer aptly calls them a "mezzanine floor") is the vista of the city below most pleasing? And the walk up which hill most delightful? Such differences amount to quibbling. How many cities can claim even one wooded path, easily climbed and only minutes away from the bustling streets, where concrete pavements give way to luxurious carpets of green, where the honking of traffic is replaced by the chirping of birds, and where the grey of stone and soot becomes the brightness of heather and blue bells, March violets and *Alpenrosen*? Those tempted to hurry the ascent will find it virtually impossible, for temptations are too many – benches for sunning, inns for refreshment, statues to contemplate, views unending.

Of these hills, the Mönchsberg constitutes the most extensive city park in Salzburg. It is made up of conglomerate stone which you will find used extensively on house facades. The Mönchsberg can be ascended in a mere 30 seconds by iron lift ("mercifully banished to the interior of the rock", sniffs Bauer), though no nature lover would admit to taking it.* As for the Kapuzinerberg (composed mostly of dolomite rock), with its stations of the cross leading up to an ancient monastery, this can only be climbed on foot; it is entered at the shopping street Linzergasse through an ancient gate, Felix Pforte. The Gaisberg ("Goat Hill"), a third peak within the city limits, is meadow-carpeted and thick with woods. It offers probably the best panoramic view of the town below and is a favorite spot for skiers who make use of hotels along the road going up the mountain. At the very top is a plain black cross with this inscription: "Thus God has loved the world."

The peak that dominates Salzburg in height and interest is the more formidable Untersberg which rises over 6000 feet to the south of town and is the source of that beautiful marble, red and also white, used lavishly in Salzburg's major buildings. Because the Untersberg is so distinctive in shape and mien, it has inspired the imagination of many visitors including, again, Franz Schubert, who spoke of its "horrible and uncanny meaning." Many legends surround the Untersberg, the best known being that Emperor Charlemagne sleeps here guarded by ravens and an army of 5000; not until his beard has grown seven times around a stone table will he awaken.

Nature did not let Salzburg down in matters of climate. Because the town is located in a basin-like valley and protected by mountains, its weather is on the whole temperate and free of the winds that sweep from the Hungarian plain to dishevel the hairdoes of Viennese ladies. For the visitor each season has its own splendor: spring fragrant with blossoms, often arriving for a short preview in February, fall similarly mild, the foliage dressed in rich burnt shades.

Summer is the most popular tourist season; if you don't mind jostling crowds and higher prices, you will delight in the pleasant days, the cool evenings. Salzburgers, not being accustomed to the

---

* That the Mönchsberg can be approached without fear today is due largely to the efforts of men known as "mountain cleaners" or "rock polishers" whose job it is to hang onto the precipices, chipping away at the rockface with hammers in order to dislodge loose stones that might otherwise cause rockslides.

stifling heat we experience in many parts of the U.S., tend to vacate the tennis courts in exhaustion when the barometer reaches 80°F.*) As for winter, when it snows – and, obligingly, it often does in time for Christmas – there is no whiter white, no greater temptation than the nearest slope. Once again Hermann Bahr said it all, remarking of the city's four seasons: "Salzburg is always beautiful, and one thinks that it is at that moment most beautiful."

Admittedly, there are two specific and less pleasant weather peculiarities in Salzburg about which it is proper to grumble. The first is *Schnürlregen* ("string rain"), so called because it comes cascading down in what appear to be strings, rather than drops. It can happen any time but is most common in the second half of August. Though residents are philosophical about the persistent wetness, the tourist office defensively prints an inordinate number of brochures which depict Salzburg in glittering sunshine. Actually, according to statistics, the city is a very respectable 16th among Austrian cities, averaging 42 inches of rain per year. Still, it's no fun for the tourist who comes for sun and receives a weeklong bath instead. One way of dealing with *Schnürlregen* is to go out and buy a Loden all-weather coat and an oversize umbrella under whose protection one can hide in some of the city's interesting museums. (The House of Nature with its dioramas of Tibet and bats and dinosaurs is a good one for such times.).

The other infamous local weather condition, which dominates the region for about 45 days per year, is called *Föhn*. Characteristic of Alpine regions, it signifies a strong, gusty, dry and warm wind which develops on the lee side of a mountain range when stable air is forced to flow over the barrier by the regional pressure gradient. Precipitation often occurs on the mountains and the air, having cooled above the condensation level, subsequently warms as it descends on the lee side with a consequent lowering of both the relative and absolute humidity. So much for science. This innocent-sounding phenomenon is suspected of causing enough maladies to lay low the entire city: from headaches to epilepsy, heart attacks to asthma. Statistics show that suicides, crimes and traffic accidents also increase under the influence of *Föhn*.

To make it more confusing, a *Föhn* day generally is visually beautiful, bringing subtropical temperatures in summer and spring balm

* Swimmers, take note: some of the nearby Salzkammergut lakes remain too cool for swimming. Mondsee is a good bet.

The bronze Celtic flagon from the Dürrnberg (Hallein, near Salzburg).

The patron saints of Salzburg Province: left St. Rupert, founder of St. Peter's Abbey and right St. Virgil who had the first cathedral built here. Schedel Chronicle (below) of the World 1493; example of the early art of bookmaking with over 1800 wood engravings, including a view of Salzburg.

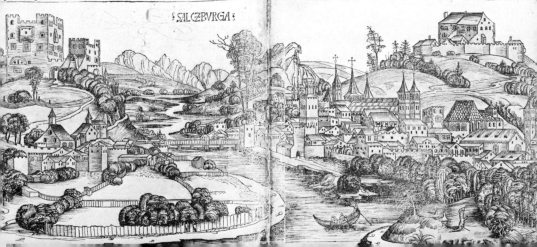

View of Salzburg with the fortress, the romanesque cathedral, the Nonnberg and the Franciscan church; second half of the 16th century, artist unknown.

St. Peter's, the oldest monastery in the German-speaking area (founded by St. Rupert) with the graveyard and rock chapel (right); Dr. Faust and Mephisto are said to have been regular drinking companions in the wine-cellar here. (The chapbook of Dr. Faust 1687).

Salzburg today.

Salzburg 150 years ago (the Sattler Panorama — on display in Café Winkler on the Mönchsberg).

St. Peter's Abbey in Salzburg contained the oldest scriptorium in Europe. The book of fraternization, the oldest work, was written here by St. Virgil (784), the chronology of the Salzburg bishops (above) and the antiphony (1160) left.

Late 16th century engraving.

Crosier from St. Peter's (11th century; the ivory crosier is older).

St. Rupert's Cross from Bischofshofen (8th century).

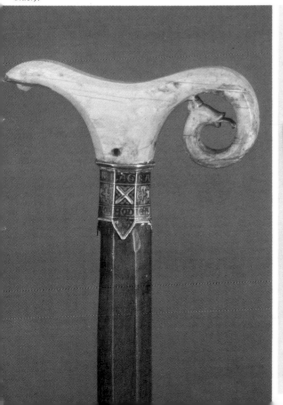

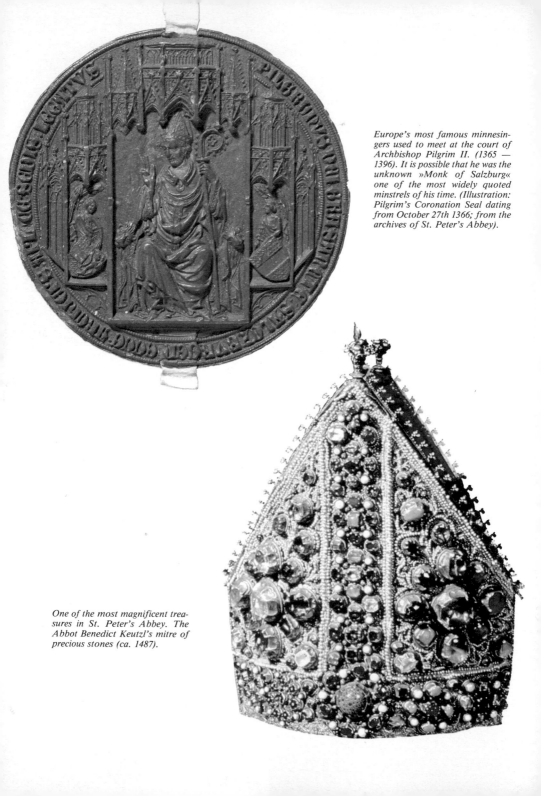

Europe's most famous minnesingers used to meet at the court of Archbishop Pilgrim II. (1365 — 1396). It is possible that he was the unknown »Monk of Salzburg« one of the most widely quoted minstrels of his time. (Illustration: Pilgrim's Coronation Seal dating from October 27th 1366; from the archives of St. Peter's Abbey).

One of the most magnificent treasures in St. Peter's Abbey. The Abbot Benedict Keutzl's mitre of precious stones (ca. 1487).

in winter. Bernhard Paumgartner, who wrote authoritatively on Salzburg, described it especially well: "In these [Föhn] conditions sensitive people wander about with frayed nerves glaring up at the wonderful silky blue sky with its wickedly fringed, glowing white clouds. On the other hand, some people attain a state of heightened consciousness during *Föhn* and can become positively meddlesome."

The spirit of any locale reflects that of its people, and Salzburg is no exception. What are they like, the residents of this venerable town? They are, of course, as diverse as one New Yorker from another, one Parisian from another. Yet to the visitor, dealing with them in a limited sphere, certain characteristics stand out. One is pride in the home town. Salzburgers in the main love Salzburg, and they are delighted when foreigners appreciate its physical beauty, its cultural richness. They express pleasure when visitors adopt such customs as the native dress – but only if that dress is accurate to tradition. (Tradition – it is a key word here, as we shall see, and not only in matters of attire.)

Business people in the city are exceedingly polite to those who enter their establishments, greeting them with a chorus of *"Grüss Gott"* (literally – "may God greet you") and issuing them out with a multi-voiced *"Danke schön, wiederseh'n."* The Salzburg business manner is formal and direct and sometimes may appear as brusque. Browsing is not customary in most shops, and bargaining is frowned upon. Efficient service is joined by an almost startling promptness. Taxicabs ordered in advance by phone will draw up at precisely the designated time – Mercedes, no less.

Salzburgers are not easy to get to know. This does not necessarily relate to the language barrier, since a large number of them, particularly those in the tourist industry, speak good English. Rather, there is a sense of privacy about residents; intimacy is reserved for their own restricted social circle. (In fact, there is in local dialect a separate word signifying the oldtime inhabitant and another word for the resident of recent immigration; the former tends to look down on the latter.)

Laws are for obeying in Salzburg. Litter is *verboten* (prohibited), hence receptacles are strategically placed and faithfully used. Policemen take a dim view of people jaywalking and have been known to lecture offenders. No parking means no parking. And if the sign says "dogs must be on a leash," there may well be a police car driving by to check things out. (This is not to say residents dislike dogs; they dote on them and take their four-legged friends everywhere – on trains, in restaurants, hairdressers, even on sightseeing boats where a dog ticket is half price.)

If you come to know a number of Salzburgers, you will doubtless find a noticeable difference between the older and younger generations. The custom of hand-kissing, for instance, a relic from the years of Viennese waltzes, champagne and crystal chandeliers, may be considered passé among the under 30s, but gentlemen of the old school stick by it faithfully, conscious of its special charm in a world singularly devoid of chivalry. Similarly, young people tend to call each other immediately by first name these days in Salzburg and to use the intimate *Du* form meaning "you" instead of the formal "you": *Sie*. But older residents often continue for a lifetime to address business associates and acquaintances in the *Sie* as *Herr* or *Frau* So-and-So. A switch to the given name and the intimate form among these traditionalists must take into consideration age, social class and specific situation and entail a regular ceremony with linked arms and emotional toasts.

Also significant in the name-calling chain is the matter of titles, and this is most confusing of all. The main thing to remember is that in Salzburg you don't give up one title for another; you just string them together. A professorship, for example, added to a doctorate, makes a Professor Dr. The clever man who has two doctorates is a D.Dr. (One of the town's most famous citizens, Nobel prize winner Friedrich von Hayek, has *four* doctorates preceding his name.) The wife, in turn, takes on her husband's honors without any scholastic effort on her own. Hence there are many honorary Frau Professors, not to be confused with the ladies who earned the titles themselves. Should this seem complicated, consider also that every *Fräulein* ("Miss") who has reached a certain, but not specified, 1) age, or 2) position, is called *Frau* ("Mrs.") whether or not she is married. As for "Ms", it's still struggling for recognition; many people in Salzburg don't even know what it means.

A final rule about titles: those relating to social position are much valued, whether or not the titles have any significance in modern times. Strictly speaking, it is illegal today to call oneself a duchess or margrave or whatever. But that doesn't matter. The fact is, in Salzburg a count counts.

Salzburgers are a mixture of country and city, homespun and sophisticated – and for good reason. During the town's rich history they have experienced a variety of sometimes contradictory influences: the rigors of daily existence in the mountain regions, the soft lives of the reigning archbishops, constantly changing national fortunes, a growing international role stemming from the Summer Festival. Such influences have affected the townspeople and have created a hybrid culture.

It is a culture of which they are proud. Unlike the residents of many cities, Salzburgers know their history. They can rattle off dates when bastions were erected, offer opinions about long past musical performances, and recite minute facts about oldtime *Trachten* ("native dress") that you will find remarkable. It follows that they also know how to savor the city's pleasures.

The visitor who wishes to partake of the native's Salzburg need only observe and imitate. Frequent the coffee shops, the beer gardens, go to a Sunday mass, climb a hill – and look. The residents do a lot of walking, "not briskly," says Bauer, "but with the leisurely and complacent gait of a landowner making a periodic inspection of his property." He studies the pastel-colored buildings, early spring wildflowers, distant peaks. He gazes at the splendor of his city floodlit at night – white marble fountains spouting water up toward a sky whose blackness is relieved by the green patina of ancient domes.

Significantly, there is an attitude of leisure here. After all, the residents of Salzburg may well have the rest of their lives to savor its delights. You and I as visitors will be moving on. We can, however, during our stay begin to understand the town's *amour propre*. For whatever mysterious combination of reasons, Salzburg *is* an enchantress.

CHAPTER ONE
ORIGINS OF "SALT CASTLE"

There are some six thousand years of man's history in the area that is now Salzburg – a history revealed in generous measure by that rich keeper of life's secrets, the soil. Within its many layers, in strict chronological progression, lie remnants of civilizations long past. Thanks to archaeologists, those diggers after ancient truths, we can today turn back the pages of time and recover Salzburg's beginnings.

The earliest traces of man date from the New Stone Age, when there was a settlement on the mountain ridge Rainberg. Life continued here during both the Bronze and Iron Ages. By 1000 B.C. a group known as Illyrians had settled on the plateau of this same mountain and given it the name Juvavum ("Seat of the God of Heaven"). Then, 500 years before Christ, the Celts invaded and developed their own fortified city, part of the Celtic kingdom of Noricum whose center lay in present-day Carinthia.

The Celts were a gifted people, erecting shelters of wood, introducing the use of iron for tools to fell men and forest, and fashioning works of art. (A magnificent bronze decanter from Celtic times was unearthed near Salzburg, and in the Nonntal district on the southern border of the city a wooden house dating from the first century A.D. has been discovered.) Most important to Salzburg's future, the Celts saw and developed the commercial possibilities which lay in salt mining, begun by the Illyrians before them. Sending the "white gold" along the river Salzach, the Celts established trading relations throughout Europe.

Salt mining remained of great importance for two milleniums.* Its vital role can be seen in the names of numerous locales that include the syllable *Salz* or *Hall*, both Celtic words for salt. Salzburg itself, meaning "Salt Castle," was the trading center of a whole area, later known as Salzkammergut ("Salt Chamber of the Crown Land") reserved for the mining and exploitation of this precious resource. Archaeologists digging in Hallstatt ("Salt City")

---

* There is a 700 year old organization of salt shippers which every June 24 (Midsummer Night's Eve) holds a ceremony on the Salzach. A straw puppet is burned as a remembrance of the years when human shippers foundering in the waters were allowed to drown as a sacrifice to the gods. Thousands of bonfires are set in wooden crates; these are sent down the river, and the shippers follow with bands playing.

have unearthed some 2,000 graves of salt miners from the early Iron Age, and in 1734 miners there discovered a Celt buried in salt, which had preserved him like a pickled fish.

Over the past few decades another important Celtic settlement has been under excavation in the town of Hallein, just a few miles outside of Salzburg, whose salt derived from the Dürrnberg mountain. One of the most important recent finds is a helmet, with a coral inlay around the tip and rim and probably worn by a prince. In the Celtic Museum in Hallein in 1980 was a special exhibition, which provided a most comprehensive study of the Celts in Central Europe.

Next on the scene after the Celts were the Romans, who occupied Juvavum in 16 B.C. Remaining for five centuries, they totalled at their height some 15,000. Like their predecessors, the Romans mined salt. They also put down a marvelous network of roads over the well worn Celtic trails. These new roads connected Juvavum not only with the salt mines but with the Romans' own country villas in outlying districts, their military camps to the north and with Rome southward. On the side of the roads ancient burying places with gifts to the dead have been found.

Roman Juvavum, the seat of a large administrative district, may well have corresponded in area to the present city. The center of the city, with its public buildings and temples, lay on the left bank of the river Salzach; its focal point, the Forum, was most likely on the site of today's Residenzplatz. Juvavum enjoyed a long period of peace. That it was quite wealthy is clear. Deep digging has brought to light parts of Roman palaces and villas with many rooms, some with magnificent tessellated floors, Theseus mosaic, and even a form of central heating. After the bombings of World War II, reconstruction of large parts of Salzburg led to the finding of a huge Roman temple, its walls more than two yards thick. An earlier digging expedition, to lay the foundation for a statue of Mozart, resulted in the excavation of a Roman floor upon which was inscribed in Latin a phrase of charming appropriateness: "Here lies happiness. Let no evil enter."

The Romans were, as a matter of fact, generally big on inscriptions, and these aid us in reconstructing their civilization. One plaque, for instance, found in a house on the street Kaigasse, tells us about a father and son whose job it was to hunt bears and other beasts for the giant amphitheater in Rome. Another one thanks the

21

administrative head of Juvavum for importing corn in a year when local prices were particularly steep.

In the fifth century A.D. the Roman adventure came to an end. Barbarian armies swept down from Bavaria, driving out the residents, and Juvavum itself was wracked by fire. Historians are not certain whether any kind of city life was salvaged or whether the area became a wood-covered ruin. Evidently, some of the sturdy Celts still survived, hiding out in the hills and eventually mingling with the invaders.

Christianity came early to the area. Contemporary accounts indicate that by the fifth century there was a Christian church with three priests here. Tradition has it that secret services, including masses and baptisms, were held in the so-called Catacombs – cave recesses carved two centuries before from the rock of the mountain Mönchsberg. The first local holy man was one Maximus who is thought to have suffered martyrdom there. At the time of the invasion of Juvavum by the barbarian armies, so the story goes, a famous Roman missionary by name of St. Severin hurried to warn the population of the advance, but Maximus, who dwelled in the Catacombs with 400 followers, was discovered and, with his group, murdered.

Such, at least, is the dramatic account you will be given by the Catacomb tour guides.* Actually, scholars are not at all sure that these were the scene of barbarian attack or even that the early Christians worshipped here. Author Alois Schmiedbauer tells us that the story seems to be based on a confusion between Juvavum and another, similar-sounding place: Joviacum, a city on the Danube.

It was to the abandoned and impoverished ghost town Juvavum that, at the end of the seventh century, an enterprising bishop named Rupert of Worms came from what is now France. Rupert had obtained permission from the Bavarian Duke to take over the district. His purpose was to bring back into the fold scattered pockets of Christianity that had survived the barbarian invasions; for such an endeavor Juvavum's location, if not its state of health, was ideal. It was during Rupert's time that the city took on its present name.

* The very existence of the Catacombs was not recognized until a terrible landslide in 1669 revealed the entrance. Over 200 people were killed and rubble was created that took a decade to clear.

22

Rupert was the first individual to gain enduring fame in Salzburg. Indeed, he is its patron saint. Having persuaded the Duke, whose name was Theodo, to present him with much of the surrounding country, including the salt mines, Rupert thus assured Salzburg's future wealth. Salt kept the town's church treasuries filled for many centuries and was the foundation of the huge fortunes of the later prince archbishops, who sometimes controlled as many as a thousand mines.

Rupert was the founder of ecclesiastical Salzburg, erecting a monastery near the fabled Catacombs in which he is said to have had his own tiny prayer cell. St. Peter's remains today the oldest continuously active monastery in the entire Latin church and the very heart of the city which grew up around it. In accordance with Benedictine custom, Rupert installed a woman, his niece Erentrudis, as abbess of the convent Nonnberg ("Nun Mountain") which he located on the foothills of the hill Burgberg. This remains, similarly, the oldest surviving religious community for women in the Latin world. Little is known about Erentrudis, though she too was later canonized.

As for Rupert, he was less beloved during his life than later. Not only the heathen tribes gave him trouble, but the Christians who were annoyed at his reforms and eventually threw him out of the city. It was not until some years after his death that the body of Salzburg's first bishop was returned to his ungrateful diocese. Today he lies in a plain, faintly illuminated stone tomb at St. Peter's Church. The date on which his relics were transferred from St. Peter's to Salzburg's Cathedral, September 24, in the year 774, is a public holiday. His niece Erentrudis is buried in the crypt of Nonnberg along with the wife of the same duke who presented Salzburg to Rupert.

Among other early bishops of note was the saintly Virgil, an Irishman noted also for his bold scientific studies. (It is said, for instance, that he insisted the world was round – an unthinkable notion which earned him the condemnation of St. Boniface, who had established the Church throughout Bavaria.) It was not uncommon for missionaries of that day, like Virgil, to venture from their Irish homeland on the treacherous journey across the Channel to western Europe. Such an expedition was an exercise in religious penitence and it held forth the reward of evangelizing pagan tribes. To be within reach of continental centers of learning as well as the famed holy places was no less an attraction, nor were the travelling missionaries unaware of the vast power wielded by royal patrons.

Virgil, known in Ireland as Fearghal, ruled Salzburg during the third quarter of the eighth century. It was he who was responsible for the construction of the town's first Cathedral on the site of a Roman basilica. A large wooden structure, it was fated to a fiery demise, as was the original St. Peter's. Virgil also supervised the building of other churches as well as houses and monasteries.

The next bishop, a distinguished scholar who founded Salzburg's library, was Arno. In the year 798, at the instigation of Charlemagne, the Holy Roman Emperor, Arno was raised by Pope Leo III to the rank of archbishop. Salzburg was thus now an archbishopric, its religious – and secular – importance greatly enhanced. By the beginning of the 9th century the town was beginning to take on its present form with the location of St. Peter's and the Cathedral already established and a parish church (St. Michael's) in existence. The burgher's quarter had a market on what is now Waagplatz and a wooden bridge led to a settlement on the other side of the river.

The Salzburg of ancient times – Celtic, Roman, early Christian – is still alive for those who wish to see it. Those interested in salt mining can tour working mines at both Hallein and Hallstatt (it's a real underground adventure, with transportation provided via raft, truck and toboggan.) Museums in these towns are rich in artifacts from the centuries of salt mining. In Salzburg the Carolino Augusteum Museum has vast holdings which span the town's 6,000 years of history; a fine collection of Roman items includes gravestones, urns and fragments of mosaic from wealthy homes.*

As for the Cathedral itself, many times rebuilt, its treasures are many, among them, the travelling flask of St. Rupert. The grave of St. Virgil is in the crypt beneath the Cathedral, and relics of this holy man are preserved, along with those of St. Rupert, in a shrine under the high altar. Statues of both saints stand on either side of the main entrance.

There are two places in Salzburg where time seems to have stood still for hundreds of years. One is St. Peter's. Though the church itself is largely baroque, the atmosphere would not appear strange

---

* Rebuilt after World War II, the Carolino Augusteum is located at Museumsplatz 6. On every floor you will find precious mementoes of Salzburgiana: items of folklore, music, sculpture, defense, home life, politics. Allow plenty of time for your visit, and ask about special exhibits.

to Rupert himself, for here the monks' "Magnificat" and "Gloria Patri" resound as they have without interruption for almost 1300 years. Here, in the Catacombs (reached by steps going up, rather than down, into the hidden darkness), one can imagine the faith of early believers penetrating the tiny, sunless rooms. And in the lovely cloister Nonnberg, at vespers the nuns still sing in unaccompanied soprano song as they did with their leader Erentrudis. They remain hidden from view, but as they kneel and rise one hears their habits rustling in the ancient stillness.

CHAPTER TWO
THE ARCHBISHOPS: MEN OF FAITH AND FOLLY

For over a thousand years it was the prince archbishops, as they were called, who ruled the city of Salzburg and the other extensive territories that fell within the archbishopric. Highly placed in the organization that was the Holy Roman Empire, they could always depend on the power of the church to back any measure, worthy or not. And because they had an important voice in the election of the emperor, they were sought after by popes and kings, taking their orders from above as it suited them and suppressing their own subjects whenever they felt the latter were assuming too many rights.

The archbishops were in charge of everything, it seemed: the area's finances, lands, armies, architecture, breweries, entertainments and, of course, the salvation of all the souls. This meant that a day in the archbishop's life was likely to entail anything from supervising the collecting of taxes (exorbitant ones) to holding mass, from dictating the price of bread or wine to ordering a palace built for a fair lady. Naturally armies were needed to defend all the archbishop's possessions and huge staffs to cater to his royal person's every whim. In effect, every resident within the archbishopric worked for him.

In family background these rulers generally were younger sons of noble families from a variety of kingdoms and principalities. Since Salzburg was not a hereditary state but an elective principality, it was the goal of every new archbishop to enhance the fame of his own house. Despite their exalted heritage and ecclesiastical garb, many were neither noble in thoughts nor religious in spirit. This is a particularly difficult concept for us to understand today when church and state are characteristically separate. But the archbishop of Salzburg up to 1803, when the area was secularized, was only secondarily a religious leader. Primarily he was a man of rank and ambition who had donned the priestly robes for the wealth and power they promised to bring. There was even one archbishop who never was ordained:*

---

* Ernst, Prince of Bavaria, unable to make up his mind to become a priest, finally abdicated.

Whether or not he came to throne with great personal wealth, the archbishop always died with it. Salt, gold, silver, iron – the area's natural resources were money in his pocket (and from the year 966 he even had the right to manufacture his own coins). Holding a monopoly on trading and mining rights, he owned thousands of farms as well as great expanses of forest and pastureland, fisheries and hunting preserves. At its peak the archiepiscopal territory extended as far north as Bavaria and south to Carinthia; this was the largest spiritual principality in the Empire.

In personality these men were as different from each other as mortals can be: some prudent and others hot-headed, this one flamboyant and that one retiring, a few who showed tolerance to other faiths and more who did not. The archbishops were free of most daily cares and struggles, and so they could also have fun, wining and dining to satiety, dancing and frolicking to their heart's content. A favorite sport was women. They may have been men of the clergy, these archbishops, and not allowed to marry, but instead they took mistresses, had mock weddings performed to salve the consciences of certain lady friends, and committed adultery with wives of court employees. Another amusement was the sport of kings: hunting. Banquets were made lively with talk of the chase, and to poach on the archbishop's preserves was about as serious an offense as one could commit, inviting such punishment as exile or slavery on a Venetian galley. Horses were treated far more kindly than the archbishop's subjects, with numerous elegant bathing pools created for their use, block-long stables to house them, and their image depicted upon frescoed walls.

It is tempting to be highly critical of Salzburg's prince archbishops, for their lives were on the whole selfish, their reigns autocratic. Yet one must not forget the other side: they were great patrons of the arts and often had superb taste in music, painting, architecture. It is largely thanks to them (and of course the gifted artisans they hired) that Salzburg is so beautiful and with so rich a cultural heritage.

As for the people who lived – and chafed – under their reign, life was not so easy. The peasants in particular had a hard time, for physical labor was arduous in the harsh mountain climate. In contrast, the burghers, most of whom were involved in trade, had a rather better life. Particularly during the 15th and 16th centuries, Salzburg was a bustling center between north and south, east and west, all the trade with Venice passing through the town. As a result, some of the citizens became quite well off with fine homes (examples of these can still be seen on streets like Kaigasse and Alter Markt). Still, all the residents were under the archbishop's thumb. Frivolity was fine for him, but woe to the peasant or burgher who indulged in too much partying, masquerading, dancing, drinking, bawdy singing – these resulted more than once in archiepiscopal decrees disallowing this or that.

In terms of political influence, the residents had none. Eventually a Rathaus ("Town Hall") was built, a golden beige building with square belfry, above whose entrance sat a figure of Justice holding an iron sword; here the Bürgermeister and town council met to discuss affairs of importance. But it was a mere gesture, for the archbishop alone made decisions – often in total disregard of the townspeople's welfare. Now and then there would occur an uprising of sorts, but after having been solidly put down by their ruler, the residents would give up, having no recourse but to grumble amongst each other and call the hated archbishop in private by appropriate nicknames.

Nor did they have any say in who would rule them next. That choice fell to the Cathedral Chapter. This body of churchmen, usually German bishops and other ecclesiastical officials of noble family, would gather at the Kapitelhaus ("Chapter House") located on the Kapitelplatz ("Chapter Square") for the momentous event. Sometimes it would be weeks or even months before the death of one archbishop and the election of another, because some of the cathedral canons might live a good distance from Salzburg, and travel was difficult.

The election procedure had great drama and was not unlike the means by which an even more powerful figure – the pope – is still chosen. To begin with, all the gates of the city were locked and a double watch posted. Business deals would halt and shops close while, within the halls of the Kapitelhaus, surrounded by guards, the haggling, politicking and compromising would begin. A certain canon would put forth one name, the emperor another, the elector of Bavaria yet a third; some choices would be sound, others ridiculous. Outside, an increasingly excited crowd would look for a pan of burning coals to be carried into the building, for that signified that the votes were being burned. Dorothy McGuigan describes the culmination: "Finally a window was flung open and one of the canons would call out, 'Long live our new Prince'". The victorious churchman was then led to the Cathedral between two rows of canons where, with a blare of trumpets and kettle-drums, he was ceremoniously seated on the Archbishop's throne. Meanwhile the city gates were flung open and messengers went flying out on horseback to bring the vital news to distant parishes."

Of the archbishops from the 8th to 15th centuries we shall speak only briefly, not because this was a dull time (battle was waged against the Magyars, Salzburg set on fire, an epidemic of the Black Plague endured) but because the period that followed is of even greater import. To give the early archbishops their due, we must first mention Gebhard who lived during an era of great hostility between emperor and pope and thought it wise to protect his domain by the building of a fortress. That monumental structure, Hohensalzburg by name, was begun in 1077 and completed centuries later; today it is one of the best preserved medieval structures anywhere in the world. Konrad I was a later archbishop who added significantly to the fortress, and another Konrad, the Third, of Wittelsbach, is remembered for his additions to Virgil's Cathedral; it was he who built the first archiepiscopal residence on the site of today's Residenz. By the end of the 13th century the town was surrounded by a stone wall for defense.

The late 14th century saw a flourishing of poetry and music under the warlike but culturally inclined Pilgrim II of Puchheim under whose reign the territorial jurisdiction of the Salzburg archbishops reached an all-time high. Pilgrim kept at his court a certain monk; we do not know his name – he was simply called "The Monk of Salzburg." We do know that his poems set to music (both worldly and religious in subject) and his playing of the guitar were masterful. The compositions that still exist by this mysterious figure who one day disappeared from the archiepiscopal court, never to return, reveal him as the last great composer of plainsong.

In 1495 there appeared on the scene one of Salzburg's most famous and, by any account, nastiest archbishops: Leonhard von Keutschach. Yet, ironically, through his very lack of scruples he helped to reinforce the town's unique and important role.

By the time he was elected, Salzburg had a substantial group of merchants, wealthy from river trade, who didn't want to be ordered around by anyone, archbishop or no. They were successful in obtaining a letter from the emperor which granted them a town council and courts, plus full rights as a city of the Holy Roman Empire. This meant, in effect, that they were placing themselves under the emperor's protection and thumbing their noses at his vassal, the archbishop. If they had succeeded, Salzburg, then basically an ecclesiastical principality with accommodation for lay servants, could have become like many German towns: a lay town with a few churches and monasteries tucked away in the corners.

Leonhard, of course, was not about to let this happen, and the means he took to prevent it can be labeled a medieval form of black comedy. He invited the mayor, sheriff and town councillors to bargain at his dinner table. They arrived in their silk and velvet robes, hungrily anticipating the hearty fare that, course after course, normally emerged from the royal kitchens. But instead they were greeted by bread, water and armed guards who bound them to sleighs – this being an icy winter night – and carried them off to nearby Radstadt. In their company during the journey was the court executioner, naked sword prominent upon his knee. Supposedly he was to have beheaded them, but influential people interceded, after which Leonhard generously gave the residents at home the chance to choose: submission to his authority or death to the dinner guests. They submitted. The next chapter is variously told: some chroniclers say the frozen group returned home alive but humbled, while others insist they all died of shock, exposure and terror.

After such a move, the archbishop obviously was not going to be very popular, so he wisely decided to remove himself from his subjects to the high fortress which he outfitted accordingly. In his spare time he oversaw the repair of the old Roman road and started his own wine house and brewery. He was a splendid administrator, his safe always full of money which he reinvested in real estate, salt and gold.

Rough, uncouth Leonhard came from a Carinthian family of minor nobility, his coat-of-arms a beetroot with leaves. There is a delightful, if fictitious, story regarding the origin of that odd trademark: when Leonhard told his farmer father he wanted to become a man of the cloth instead of the till, Papa, angered, threw a beetroot at him.

The successor to Leonhard von Keutschach, Matthäus Lang, was a well educated man, scrupulous, independent of mind, and a confidant of the Habsburg emperor Maximilian I. Lang did not appreciate the excesses of the clergy to which he belonged, writing in one pastoral letter of their "dissolute" life, their "unrestrained and disgraceful deeds." "They dress like laymen," he wrote, "... indulge in drink and revels, blasphemies and quarrels, and then, drunk with sleep and reeking of wine, they approach the altar."

Lang began his rule in a rather tolerant frame of mind, even toward Protestantism which then was gathering adherents quickly. But as events occurred within the archbishopric that revealed the disinclination of the populace to accept without question his own infallibility, he tightened his control and became far less benevolent to Protestants and everyone else.

Leonhard von Keutschach had faced his challenge in Salzburg's middle class burghers; Matthäus Lang, in contrast, had to deal with the peasants who found the heavy taxation intolerable. Their anger having reached breaking point in 1525, they rose in rebellion against the archbishop. It was the night of June 5. Drums beating, mountain fires blazing and bells ringing, the peasants approached from the different areas of his domain – the Pongau, Gastein, Radstadt – entering the city through the Stein Gate. Lang fled to the fortress while the peasants invaded the Residenz, destroying its possessions and banqueting on its food. With wooden cannons they answered the thunderous artillery emanating from the Festung. It went on like this for three months, Lang waiting nervously for help from his high retreat. This was the only time in its entire life of 900 years that the strength of Hohensalzburg was tested. From the beginning the chances of victory by the peasants were slim, for they were badly armed and the fortress was well nigh unapproachable. From there the archbishop had tunnels dug into town, enabling him to receive constant stores of food; a great cistern gathered rainwater for his use. And powerful help did eventually come to him in the form of Ludwig, Prince of Bavaria, a staunch Catholic who sent an army of 8000. The peasants retreated.

It was Lang's turn to retaliate. He filled the dungeons with peasant rebels, built a series of bastions around Hohensalzburg and, when yet another rebellion occurred the following spring, had his mercenaries capture and murder the peasants by the thousands. From then on he was able to devote himself to the improvement of education and road building – more agreeable tasks. He died in 1540.

In 1587, with the ceremony that, after a series of political maneuvers, elevated 28 year-old Wolf Dietrich von Raitenau to the archiepiscopal throne, the years of Salzburg's greatest glory and power began. Wolf Dietrich and the two Renaissance princes that followed him transformed it from a dark and cramped medieval town into the glittering showplace it remains to this day.

Wolf Dietrich came to Salzburg having been educated in the splendor of Renaissance Rome. And educated he was, with a keen mind, strong cultural interests, and the ability to speak six languages without accent. His heritage was a proud one: German warrior father, mother related to the Medicis. Of a compact figure and sporting a closely trimmed beard, Wolf Dietrich was characteristically attired in a plumed Spanish hat, black cape, a rapier at his side (he did agree to leave the rapier outside the church). This appearance revealed clearly the secular person he was – indeed, Wolf Dietrich was not even ordained until after taking over the archbishopric.

He was not the kind of man with whom people felt comfortable, nor did he much care how they felt. He was stubborn, intolerant, cunning, hot-tempered, and desirous of keeping his distance from those beneath him while availing himself fully of their services; on one occasion he travelled to Regensburg with 410 persons and 324 horses.

Only one person did Wolf Dietrich really love, and that was Salome Alt. She was of a respected and wealthy merchant family and considered to be the most beautiful young woman in town. The archbishop may have met her at her father's house or at a wedding held in a tavern. But wherever they first set eyes on each other, theirs was a lifelong union which resulted in some 15 children. Early on in the relationship either a mock or real wedding took place with a chaplain officiating.

Salome lived in a wing of the building adjoining the Franciscan Church which connected with Wolf Dietrich's chambers through a door hidden by a wardrobe. A certain tower was pulled down because it afforded curious townspeople too much opportunity for spying. Eventually Wolf Dietrich built for Salome a fine country seat across the river, naming it Altenau; here she lived quietly, more and more removing herself from public view. Salome Alt seems to have had a positive influence on the fiery archbishop, causing him to develop a more tolerant view on such subjects as Protestantism. Toward her and the children, ten of whom lived to maturity, he was always loving. Salome was eventually elevated to the nobility by the emperor.

What set Wolf Dietrich apart from all those who came before and after him was far more than his theatrical personality and his scanda-

Prince Archbishops of Salzburg: Leonhard von Keutschach.

Kardinal Matthäus Lang von Wellenburg.

Marcus Sitticus von Hohenems.

Paris Graf Lodron.

Interior of Salzburg Cathedral (1682).

Ceremonial procession of an archbishop with his royal household (ca. 1710).

Salomé Alt. *Prince Archbishop Wolf-Dietrich von Raitenau.*

Mirabell Palace (formerly Altenau) which Wolf-Dietrich had built for Salomé Alt.

The Cathedral, adjoined by the former royal archiepiscopal residence; in the state rooms of this building opera was performed for the first time north of the Alps. In the middle of the »Residenz« Square is the horse fountain and on the other side is the New »Residenz« with the Glockenspiel tower. (below).

EFIGIES AVREOLI THEOPHRASTI AB HOHEN
HEIM SVE ÆTATIS 47

Wolf Dietrich's mausoleum in the St. Sebastian graveyard; the famous physician Paracelsus is also buried here. He lived and worked in Salzburg in the years 1524 and 1541.

The archiepiscopal summer riding school, now part of the festival complex, is the oldest of its kind in Europe.

Ansicht der Hochfürstlich Salz-   burgischen Somer Reutschule.

Sr. Excellenz Dem Hochgebohrnen Herrn, Herrn   Leopold Joseph des H. R. R. Graf von Kuenburg
freyherrn zu Kunegg, Jung Woschitz, Mittschin u. Hamberg im Konig.   reich Böheim, dann Grafenau im hohen Erzstift Salzburg, Sr. K. K. M.
würckl. Kämerer, auch Sr. Hochfürstl. Gnaden Erzbischof zu Salzburg würckl.   geheimen Rath, Obrist Stallmaistern, Einer Hoch. Landschaft verordneten

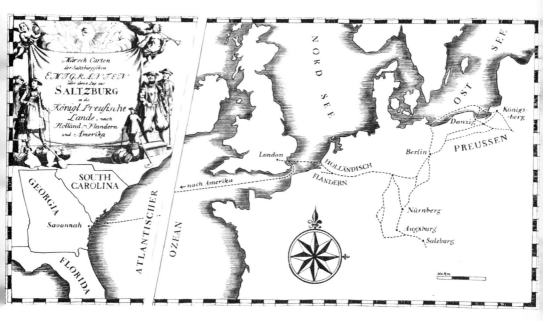

The March of the Salzburg Emigrants

In 1981 an exhibition was held in Goldegg Castle, about 50 miles south of Salzburg, to commemorate the emigration of over 21,000 Protestants from the city and province of Salzburg, forced to leave because of their religious beliefs and exchange their settled homeland for an uncertain future in foreign parts. Those who suffered most were the farmers and in the winter of 1731 alone, 4,184 emigrated, leaving behind 1,776 farms. Augsburg was the principle stopping point for emigrants before they went on either to Eastern Prussia, Holland or America. They were particularly welcomed in the English colony of Georgia, where General James Oglethorpe had founded the city of Savannah with deported convicts and needed trustworthy, industrious and honest persons to reinforce border posts in the Spanish-American war against the English. 42 families accepted the invitation, their passage from Rotterdam was approved and paid for by the English Parliament. From Augsburg the journey lasted 143 days, 67 of which were spent at sea. They landed in Savannah in March 1734 and founded the settlement Ebenezer, which grew rapidly. In the following year another 57 Salzburgers arrived.

Though the town of Ebenezer no longer exists, one can still visit the large brick Jerusalem Church which in its present form dates back to 1763. The oldest church in Georgia, it was built by the Salzburg emigrants with the help of patrons from the European cities of Frankfurt, London, Augsburg and Halle. It was used by the British during the American Revolution, first as a hospital and then as a stable. There is also a Salzburg emigrant's house in this area which was brought here from an outlying district and a Lutheran retreat used particularly by business people from Atlanta.

Descendants of the original Salzburgers still live in the area formerly known as Ebenezer. Most of them are small-hold farmers who have retained many of the habits and customs of their alpine past and they look upon their Salzburg lineage with great pride.

A distinguished American professor of history, George Fenwick Jones, who is from Savannah and whose ancestors worked closely with the early Lutheran emigrants, has added greatly to our knowledge of this group. He is the translator, editor and annotator of a multi-volume series of reports sent from Ebenezer in the first half of the eighteenth century after the Protestants had been expelled from Salzburg in 1731. The reports were sent to the Francke Foundation in Halle, Germany for publication to gain support for the settlers.

Leopoldskron Palace was the home of one of the founders of the Salzburg Festival, Max Reinhardt, not the Trapp Family who lived in a villa in Aigen (below left). The gazebo, now situated opposite Leopoldskron Palace was also created by Hollywood. It is visited annually by thousands of tourists.

lous union. It was, rather, the marvelous imagination and the courage he had to carry out his dreams. Wolf Dietrich was a man possessed of a vision: Salzburg reborn, with noble buildings and open spaces. For him the town was little more than a giant piece of clay which he wanted to mold into something greater. For this he had the help of an equally big thinker: the Italian artist and town planner of European reputation, Vincenzo Scamozzi. In the winter of 1603–4 Scamozzi explained to the archbishop his concept of an ideal city with its five centrally situated and spacious squares on which would stand lofty churches and palaces. Wolf Dietrich responded fully, and soon what had been on paper was taking form.

Their first task was to tear down the undesirable. When the lovely romanesque cathedral began to burn, therefore, Wolf Dietrich was not displeased and made no effort to halt the conflagration; in fact, rumors were heard that he had started the fire himself. Then the church graveyard had to be moved across the river to make room for the handsome square that would become Residenzplatz. Some 55 residents' homes were demolished (for these the people did receive full compensation), creating an acute housing shortage that was somewhat eased when the archbishop moved the city walls outward and opened the street Griesgasse. It was in all an effort shocking in its audacity, yet planned with undeniable artistry.

And then Wolf Dietrich began to build where he had torn down: the Residenz, the magnificent-block-long court stables, the Capuchin monastery, the chapel and cloister of St. Sebastian's cemetery with the Gabriel chapel, the Chapter House. How far he would have gone with more time one can only guess, but his leadership came to a sudden end in 1612.

In his lust for power the archbishop had picked a quarrel with the Elector of Bavaria over some unimportant mining rights. Long since in trouble with bishops and even the pope over matters ranging from his family life to his temper, he was now without allies and uncharacteristically fearful. Unwilling to wait out the storm, he tried to flee from the archbishopric, sending Salome, children, servants and jewels off first in a van of carriages. Following her, he was caught by Bavarian troops who were assisted by none other than his own nephew, Markus Sittikus by name. Brought back to Salzburg, Wolf Dietrich was made prisoner in the very fortress that was built to offer protection to those of his position. Sittikus was thereupon elected to succeed him.

In Hohensalzburg Wolf Dietrich remained for five years, gradually weakened by attacks of epilepsy. Salome retired, grief-stricken, to Wels, where through the intercession of the abbess at Nonnberg Convent, she was at least enabled to write her luckless lover. Wolf Dietrich died in 1617 after five years of captivity, his last wish being in stark contrast to his flamboyant life: he asked to be buried in the dark of night, escorted by only six Franciscan friars. But such was not to be. An archbishop in life, even one deposed and jailed, was destined for a glorious death.

Today Wolf Dietrich lies in the mausoleum he himself designed. Once again there is an appropriate, though apochryphal, story that he was lowered into the grave in an upright position, holding in his hands architectural plans.

Salome lived to the age of 65, true to her love until the end. Writes Liselotte von Eltz-Hoffmann: "She had in her life come to know what Wolf Dietrich at the time of his arrest wrote on the wall at the fortress of Werfen: 'Love is the beginning of suffering – in a short while or later.'"

After a while, the Salzburgers began to grumble about their new leader, Markus Sittikus von Hohenems. Well, they said, at least Wolf Dietrich had only one mistress; Markus Sittikus has *two*. In fact, he probably had more than two, judging by his pleasure-happy attitude and the goldsmiths' bills he accrued for ladies' jewelry. The supreme example of his obsession with fun and games lies in the palace he built called Hellbrunn, which we shall visit later in this text. Suffice it to say here that if a serious word or thought entered the conversation in this fantasy-land of fountains and romance, it must have been quickly squelched.

When he wasn't being a playboy, Markus Sittikus was working with gusto at the religious side of life, celebrating daily masses, founding pious brotherhoods, and forbidding Lutherans to engage in trade – he took over all the mining interests they'd owned. The new archbishop also did a lot of building beyond the *Lustschloss* ("pleasure palace") variety. For one, he discarded Wolf Dietrich's Cathedral plans, drew up new ones along with fire regulations, and laid the foundation stone; he finished one wing of the Residenz along with its New Building; he remodeled Salome Alt's castle (so distasteful did he find it that he renamed it Mirabell – some say after a lady of that name); in addition he erected several churches and city gates. In all it was quite an output for a mere seven years' rule.

When we talk of Markus Sittikus we must point to yet another

34

aspect of his reign, perhaps the most important: his great love of theater and music. It was he who brought the first performance of Italian opera to German soil, in 1617; the location for the performance was an outdoor theater that he created at his own Hellbrunn.

Paris Lodron, who next took over at the age of 33, was the greatest archbishop of them all. If less charismatic a personality than Wolf Dietrich, he was more mature and had a gentle, kindly disposition.

Lodron was noted for his integrity and peace-loving nature. Elected at the beginning of the Thirty Years War which broke out as a religious contest between Catholics and Protestants, he managed to keep Salzburg clear of the hostilities by maintaining a strict neutrality. Preserving the religious freedom of those within his realm, he allowed neither the armies of the Catholic League nor the Jesuits to enter the archbishopric. This was not easy, for pope and emperor both courted him, hoping he would be tempted to take measures on their behalf. To strengthen his domain Paris Lodron built a mighty series of ramparts, towers and gates on the Kapuzinerberg, the Mönchsberg and at Hohensalzburg. A large and well equipped army numbering 20,000 was on command, and the archbishop himself often inspected the guards upon the bastions. At the end of the war Salzburg was still an oasis of peace and plenty amidst the charred landscape of central Europe.

Paris Lodron's coat-of-arms, the lion with the knotted tail, can be found all over town, for while "Wolf Dietrich glimpsed Salzburg, Paris Lodron carved the vision in stone . . . " (Hermann Bahr). It was he who finished the Cathedral and opened it in 1628 to great fanfares and the Missa Salisburgensis written by Heinrich Ignaz Franz Biber. Posted in various galleries of the sumptuous church were eight choirs singing a total of 16 parts; 34 instrumental parts and three organs accompanied them.* This rich musical fare was accompanied no less grandly by eight days of feasting and revelry. In all it was one of the most elaborate extravaganzas ever recorded, marking the start of Salzburg's traditional association with church music.

In 1628 came another big event, permission from the emperor and pope to raise the status of the local Catholic school founded by Markus Sittikus to that of a university, named after Paris Lodron.

---

* Accounts differ, some more grandiose than others; the one given above is by Marboe. Rickett adds that there were three groups of trumpets and drums alone.

This became a spiritual center of Catholic southern Germany, known for its library and fine theatrical performances. Among other projects for which Paris Lodron can be credited are the Loreto Church and the completion of the Residenz.

He lived in a manner no less lavish than the spectacles he staged, this last archbishop of truly grand style. McGuigan tells us he was attended by "twelve boys of noble family dressed as pages in red velvet and 14 lords-chamberlain, each of whom carried an enormous gold key as a sign of his office. Guarding his person were 30 Carabinieri on foot, and when he went on a journey, an additional 50 mounted arquebusiers. Hundreds of servants waited on him in the Palace, all clad in the livery of the Court, blue with red facings." He hired "ordinary bathers" and "master bathers", normal cooks and chefs who prepared his food alone.

Just to be sure that he'd not be short of qualified estate managers, Paris Lodron set up a boys' school to train them. Nor did he neglect his relatives. For his brother's family he built a whole complex of palaces complete with stables, bakeries and breweries at what is now Makartplatz. Most of his own leisure time was spent at Mirabell which he loved and where he entertained important visitors with week-long processions, theater, fireworks and balls in which the entire city took part.

In the year 1653 Paris Lodron died at Schloss Mirabell. He was buried under the dome of the Cathedral, and his heart was placed beside that of a monk at the Capuchin monastery whose friendship and counsel he had often sought. On his passing, Salzburg, at the peak of her fame and influence, mourned him like a child the father.

Guidobald Count Thun who, as bishop of Regensburg, resided in that town more than he did in Salzburg, added some finishing touches to the loveliness his three predecessors had wrought. He is often referred to as the lover of fountains, for whenever he found an appropriate empty space he would commission that cheerful touch from the south. (Of these, the finest is on the Residenzplatz.)

Horses were also big in his life. It was Guidobald Thun who was responsible for the Winter Riding School, formerly the Stadt Saal ("City Room") and now the "Karl Böhm Saal", whose surrealistic ceiling frescoes, implemented some years later by the court painter Rottmayr, depict riders slicing off the heads of Turks. A wonderful inscription in this area of the festival complex reminds us a bit defensively that "so that ... no mean grumbler should consider the size of the building extravagant, Guidobald, Archbishop and Prince, used the cut-off rock in mighty blocks for churches in the year of Our Lord 1662."

Guidobald was a big, lusty man of great strength and appetite. Once out hunting with a party of German princes, he was said to have grabbed and held a running boar by its bristles. Queen Christine of Sweden wrote home about him: "The Archbishop is celebrated among his peasants because he can drink a whole keg of wine without getting drunk, and any man who drinks less is counted a blockhead."

During Guidobald's reign some unusually big natural disasters occurred. First the river Salzach flooded the whole valley near Hallein; then a hurricane hit Salzburg, throwing down roofs and steeples of churches as if they were made of paper. Also in his time came that terrible avalanche from the Mönchsberg which killed over two hundred people.

Guidobald's own demise was an unlikely one for such a hearty man: he broke through a little bridge at Schloss Hellbrunn while feeding fish in a brook, and gangrene set in.

His successor, Maximilian Gandolf von Kuenberg, was one of three archbishops from a Carinthian noble family. He was a thoroughly unsavory man under whose rule the area's Protestants once again found themselves in trouble, many being forced to flee. He also held many trials in which innocent people, including children, were convicted and killed by burning, hanging or guillotine. At the corner of Paris-Lodron- and Wolf-Dietrich-Strasse there stood a concrete sign of Max Gandolf's evil-doing: the so-called "Witches' Tower." With the prisons full, those accused of witchcraft and sorcery were locked up here. But because the superstitious folk believed that witches could make themselves invisible if their feet were allowed to touch the ground, the accused could not be thrown into an ordinary prison. Instead they were strung up in great copper kettles suspended from the ceiling with food shoved in to them on sticks.

During Max Gandolf's reign a huge Turkish army marched up through Hungary and besieged Vienna, threatening all of Europe with Mohammedanism. Salzburg, which had long lived in fear of the "terrible Turks," found itself full of rich Viennese nobility in search of refuge. Every morning all the church bells would ring and the populace was required to pray on their knees for the Turks' defeat. Max Gandolf sent a token number of men and weapons to battle the infidels whose siege of Vienna was eventually broken. The cowardly Viennese nobility returned home after leaving costly gifts of thanks in the pilgrimage church of Maria Plain which had been built by Maximilian in one of his quieter moments. He was responsible, too, for the earlier stages of the Cajetan church and the tower of the beautiful Mülln church. That a human so committed to the ill treatment of others could participate in the creation of fine places of worship may seem paradoxical but it was a commonplace fact of life in those times. More true to character, Max Gandolf added substantially to Salzburg's defense through bastions upon the Hohensalzburg.

Next, another Thun was head of the archbishopric: Johannes Ernst Count Thun, stepson of Guidobald. His role in building was very important. Indeed, he was the archbishop most intimately involved with that great Austrian architect, Fischer von Erlach. Under Johann Thun's direction, Fischer created some of Salzburg's most famous buildings, including the University or Collegiate Church, Ursuline Church and Holy Trinity Church. Johann Thun also ordered a seven-towered castle to be torn down, and on the site Fischer von Erlach built St. John's Hospital* and Chapel as a refuge for pilgrims, priests, impoverished students and other poor. When the hospital was opened, the archbishop washed the feet of the first pilgrim. Schloss Klesheim, which suffered a time of notoriety centuries later under Hitler, was begun by this same team. Thun was responsible, too, for the purchase of the delightful Glockenspiel which to this day plays atop the New Building of the Residenz. Under this enthusiastic patron, Fischer rebuilt the archbishop's stables and transformed what had been a quarry in the Mönchsberg into an open-air theater of stone: the Felsenreitschule, or Summer Riding School.

Thun was a vigorous, strong-willed ascetic and an able businessman whose enormous wealth resulted largely from investments in the Dutch East India Company.

Afterward came Franz Anton Count Harrach, who immediately dismissed the great Fischer von Erlach. For such projects as his remodeling of Schloss Mirabell he chose a lesser but gifted architect,

---

* In the Middle Ages Salzburg had a Citizens' Hospital and Chapel to St. Blasius, built under the archbishop Friedrich III in the 14th century. Today one can see its courtyard, situated behind the church, with triple rows of arcades built up against the Mönchsberg; restored, with window boxes, it is a lovely sight.

Lukas von Hildebrandt, whose work – if not so lofty and idealistic as Fischer's – was more elegant and pleasing to the average eye.

Next on the scene was an archbishop remembered to posterity for a particularly ugly deed. Leopold Anton Freiherr von Firmian was nicknamed "The Huntsman" with good reason, for his prey included people as well as game. It was he who in 1731–2 tossed out from the archbishopric from 20,000 to 30,000 Protestants (reports differ), leaving the area, in the words of Will Durant, "thoroughly and theocratically Catholic."

Europe had long been involved in the struggle between Catholics and Protestants.* The Reformation, which spread Martin Luther's teaching throughout northern Europe, was answered by the Catholics in the form of the Counter-Reformation, an attempt both to cleanse the church of some of its excesses and to eradicate Protestantism. The Treaty of Westphalia in 1648, which brought the religious wars to a conclusion, left to each reigning prince the decision as to what religions would be practised and tolerated in his realm. In Leopold Firmian's time the Lutherans of the area had been assured the support of nearby Protestant princes and hence felt quite confident; they had even formed their own "Salt League" which met freely. Obviously they did not count on the hatred of their prince archbishop who, encouraged by his wily chancellor (the Italian Christiani) and loath to lose the pope's favor by tolerating Protestantism, decided to rid the territory of these "heathen." His means was to declare that a meeting of the Salt League was, in fact, a "revolution" and to ask the help of the emperor to suppress it. This accomplished, he issued an edict announcing the expulsion of the Protestants from Salzburg. Thus began an period of terror, with old and sick, infants and elderly driven like cattle across Bavaria; the districts they left became like ghost towns.

The homeless residents of Salzburg emigrated where they could, and those who survived set up new lives in the Netherlands, East Prussia, England, South Germany and the United States. The group that came to America settled mostly in Georgia, creating the town of Ebeneezer. The story of their arrival and adjustment is as dramatic as any in the annals of colonial America: weary trips on foot to

---

* In fact, one of Salzburg's lesser-sung heroes was involved directly in this struggle. He was miner Joseph Schaitberger, born in the mid 17th century at Hallein, and condemned by the court as a heretic for his beliefs as expressed in the "Protestant's Confession of Faith."

the European port, illness-ridden, storm-filled sea voyages, arrival in a strange land, dealings with local Indians, the establishment of farms, schools, churches, orphanages and industry, eventual participation in the Revolutionary War.*

With the Lutherans out of his archbishopric, Leopold Firmian could concentrate on more pleasant matters. Among these were improvements to the ornamental horse trough on Sigmundsplatz (with frescoed horses behind a Neptune statue, it is an inspired creation) and the building of Schloss Leopoldskron. The latter project was intended to uplift his family's flagging social standing; a masterly creation by a Scottish Benedictine, it remains Leopold Firmian's claim to fame of a more positive variety, revealing his zest for learning and love of art, as well as his obsession with things astrological. Here he lived, recluse-like, until his death of a violent hemorrhage in 1744.

In 1753 the archbishopric was taken over by a man kindly remembered to this day for one special deed: he treated Wolfgang Amadeus Mozart, who worked in his court, with respect and courtesy – no small thing in the days when a musician was but a servant. Sigismund von Schrattenbach is also credited with directing a dramatic feat of engineering and art: the creation of the Neutor ("New Gate"). This was a tunnel breaking directly through the rock of the Mönchsberg, thus linking the town with the outlying Riedenburg district. In the preceding century an attempt had been made to cut the mountain from the top down but this did not prove feasible, and it was under Sigismund that the digging was conducted from both sides of the rock, with speedy (two years) and precise results.** On the city side the round opening of the gate is bordered by streaked pilasters featuring the heads of Medusas. At the top of the arch in a wreath is a portrait of the archbishop, above which a flat ornamental top plate is inscribed, in Latin, with these words: "The stones speak of thee." (Salzburg's archbishops were not noted for modesty or anonymity.) The Riedenburg side is decorated by the huge figure of an ancient warrior surrounded by war trophies and burning bullets.

* For a stirring account of this migration and of the birth, life and death of Ebeneezer, see Strobel's book *The Salzburgers and Their Descendents*. The great German author Goethe used the expulsion of the Protestants fictionally in his epic poem *Hermann and Dorothea*.

** The residents weren't so quick to appreciate the Neutor, however, being convinced that if they groped their way through it late at night they would be sure to develop pneumonia.

The man who next donned the purple robes was Hieronymus von Colloredo. Acutely intelligent, admiring of the new, enlightened ideas of Voltaire and Rousseau, this ruler was, however, thoroughly autocratic in his own realm. Similarly, though he was able, through a series of edicts regulating taxes, to put the then foundering archbishopric on a much sounder financial footing, he was himself avaricious to the core.

Hieronymus probably would have settled into some dusty niche of history were it not for his connection with two remarkable, small-statured men: one was Mozart, the other Napoleon. Mozart worked for Hieronymus as he had for Sigismund, but here the similarity ended. Hieronymus von Colloredo had no real regard for his servant and, in fact, made it clear that he considered Mozart's talent to be piddling. The disenchanted composer left his employer – and Salzburg – forever (alas, forever was to be short, for he died at the age of 35).

As for Napoleon, Emperor of the French, it was due to him that the long line of Salzburg's prince archbishops came to a sudden and ignominious end. When the French army invaded Salzburg under Napoleon's leadership, there was little purpose in resisting the huge force. The fortress was handed over to his men: the first and only foreign invasion in its history. Hieronymus, untouched by traits of the hero or martyr, simply fled to Vienna, but not before he'd packed up some of the city's choice items of art.

The Salzburg he left was looted and damaged disgracefully. Residents, taking their erstwhile leader's cue, began to leave in droves. Politically, by the Treaty of Lunéville in 1801, Salzburg was secularized and given over to the emperor's brother, the Elector of Bavaria, Grand Duke Ferdinand, as compensation for his loss of Tuscany. The Duke took a lot that Hieronymus had left behind in the way of treasures of art (and there was a lot to take, since the archbishops for centuries had vied with each other in contributions to the splendor of their court). Some of these ended up in Florence. Others were lost and never found, among them silverware for 1200 from the time of Wolf Dietrich.

Safe in Vienna, Hieronymus von Colloredo could have helped his onetime archbishopric, but he didn't. Having previously deposited in a Viennese banking house the money that had resulted from his financial stringency measures, he not only refused to pay any share of the war costs but extracted additional payments from the city.

With all the money, he put together a luxurious court in Vienna where, for a time, he pretended to rule.

There is a peculiar justice in the fact that the same archbishop who had a musical genius kicked out of his home town (literally kicked out, as we shall see later) was himself unceremoniously deposed by a military genius.

Speaking of Napoleon, he had a Salzburg connection of another variety which residents there still love to talk about. She was a blonde beauty named Emilie Wolfsberg who took to accompanying Napoleon on military campaigns dressed as a man. Supposedly she bore him a child. Napoleon made her a wealthy baroness but, after his exile, failed to recognize her. She ended up in the Salzburg suburb of Gnigl where she was widowed twice, living out her days in the company of about 30 dogs who ate from silver dishes and slept on silken cushions. Emilie died mentally deranged and penniless. Her grave can be seen today in the Gnigl cemetery. They call her "The Countess with the Dogs."

To this day Salzburg has an archbishop; he lives in a palatial residence on Kapitelplatz and he is still considered the papal legate. His power, however, is largely confined to matters spiritual. In the end, perhaps that is best. Judging by Salzburg's thousand years of archiepiscopal rule, it is awfully hard to be rich and powerful while maintaining one's religious scruples.

CHAPTER THREE
THE BLEAK AND BRIGHT OF MODERN TIMES

So ended Salzburg's long line of prince archbishops. Bereft of power and riches, the town would have to wait many decades for a resurgence of old glory in a new form.

For the present, however, life was pretty bleak. No longer a focal point of history, Salzburg turned into a sleepy farming community, cows grazing over the once proud Residenzplatz, mansions empty, the fortress become a barracks. The city's very nationality, the boundaries of its land, changed with confusing rapidity. By 1805, with the Treaty of Pressburg, Salzburg was for the first time given over to Austria which then was not a nation but a powerful multinational empire, presided over by the Habsburg dynasty. As part of the province Upper Austria, Salzburg was not even first city; this honor went to Linz. Within the next decade, the former archbishopric was bounced to France, made a Bavarian province and returned to Austria. Shorn of territory (Berchtesgaden and Reichenhall), trade curtailed, university suppressed, mint closed, treasures of canvas, silver and gold spirited off to foreign lands, Salzburg was treated roughly by the gods as well as man: in 1818 a great fire destroyed 74 houses on the right bank of the Salzach.

To Vienna had gone all the privileges of the former archbishopric, including control of the salt mines and trade. Indeed, it was Vienna (with Budapest following close behind) which was the star metropolis of the Habsburg Empire during the 19th century. To this era of creative brilliance, of pomp and frivolity and theatrics, many Austrians look back nostalgically even today. And no wonder. The likes of Johann Strauss, Sr. and Jr., of Gustav Mahler, of Sigmund Freud, Arthur Schnitzler, Gustav Klimt, are not encountered every day.

By the latter part of that century, however, things were looking up in Salzburg. The town, which had always had a strong musical tradition, began to realize that its native son Wolfgang Amadeus Mozart was a lot more talented than his contemporaries had thought and that his shining image might do something for the city's tarnished one; a first festival of Mozart's music was presented in 1842, at which time a statue was erected in his honor. Painters, too, were discovering and recording the town's charms, and before long tourism – which formerly had been a pursuit of just the nobility – was a growing industry. As an independent province of the Austro-Hungarian (formerly Habsburg) Empire, Salzburg was given its own provincial government. An important district between Mirabell Palace and the Linzer Gate was added to the town by Emperor Franz Joseph, and a railway connecting Salzburg with Vienna and Munich and, later, Innsbruck, made it much more accessible. Very little building had been done in the years preceding, so the new rail station was heralded as a major event, a signal that Salzburg had a future, after all.

But once again war intruded: World War I, which resulted in 1918 in the break-up of the Austro-Hungarian Empire and the formation of the Austrian nation. Of the 49,000 people from Salzburg who served in the army during this dark time, 6,000 were killed in action. The end of the hostilities brought a strong desire for beauty: catharsis through a flowering of the arts. Berlin was a focus of such creativity; so was Salzburg. The latter's now famous summer festival, begun in 1920, and the companion festivals that grew up later around it became Salzburg's chief attraction, turning it into a center for the sophisticated performer and listener.

After this burgeoning of the arts, there came a sudden hiatus in 1938 when Adolf Hitler, from his home in nearby Berchtesgaden, decreed the union of Austria with Germany: *Anschluss*.

The relationship between these two peoples before, during and after the sorry days of World War II is a complex one, not readily understood even by historians. Reduced to a truncated version of its former greatness by the post-World War I peace settlement, Austria had found it extremely difficult to discover a sense of nationhood separate from the Empire, whose glorious mission had been to defend western civilization from the Turks and Slavs to the east. There did remain the possibility of union with Germany, something that substantial numbers of people had desired even during the Habsburg years. Since all the non-German speaking portions of the realm had formed independent nations after the war, there was even more reason for joining with Germany, with whom Austria had a language and cultural heritage in common. But historical tensions made this an uneasy choice. Austria regarded itself as a Catholic nation in contrast to a predominantly Protestant Germany. And the little rump state did not feel at one with a Prussianized German regime that, under the leadership of Bismarck, the "Iron Chancellor", had waged war on the Habsburg Empire in 1866 for the purpose of expelling it from the German Confederation.

When the Nazis came to power in Germany in 1933, many Austrians – including some who previously had desired union with Germany – discarded their pan-German sentiments and hastened to try and save their nation from Hitler's definition of *Anschluss* with its new and ugly connotations. To no avail. Chancellor Engelbert Dollfuss was murdered by the Nazis for such an attempt, and his successor Kurt von Schuschnigg fared little better, being forced by Hitler to resign on the eve of the German invasion of Austria in 1938.

The *Führer* (literally, "leader") arrived triumphantly in Salzburg March 13, 1938, after a series of military breakdowns on the road to Austria. He had selected it as a major rail head – a supply base for his huge war machine. In providing much needed jobs, Hitler gained many adherents, Austria being then in the throes of economic depression. One cannot doubt that Nazism found many fanatic followers in Salzburg, as it did in Vienna. But Hitler hated the Austrian capital for its ethnically and culturally mixed character, whereas Salzburg he considered to be racially "pure"; hence he chose it to be a center for his Thousand Year *Reich*.

Whatever the sentiments of the people toward the *Führer*, loyalty was not only expected of them; it was demanded. The "Aryan" artist who refused to submit his brush and palette to the nationalistic goals of the Nazi party, the worker who would not issue the Nazi salute, were risking job and even life. But there were some who took such chances – especially Socialists, spreading anti-Nazi information, storing arms for use against Nazi Germany and befriending Jews. Of three significant Socialist resistance groups, Salzburg's was one. Unfortunately, the whole network was discovered and crushed.

Salzburg did not have many Jewish residents even before the consummation of Anschluss; there were 161 on record in 1938. Anti-Semitism here, as elsewhere in Europe, had taken its toll through the centuries. In the year 803 the first Jews, mainly merchants and physicians, were permitted to settle in the town. According to an old chronicle, by 1349 a great persecution had occurred, with 1200 of them massacred; they were charged with having caused the black death by poisoning the fountains. Later, a mass burning took place at the Mülln church and in nearby Hallein. Under the infamous Leonhard von Keutschach Jews were banished from Salzburg "forever and all time," accused of having stolen a golden monstrance from Nonnberg abbey. But there were also periods of tolerance, the most notable one being under the 15th century reign of Archbishop Johann II of Reisberg and another occurring during the rule of Archbishop Hieronymus Colloredo (the same gentleman who exhibited rather less tolerance to Mozart). Even during the better times, however, Jews had to live in a separate area, Judengasse, and were required to reveal their presence elsewhere, men by wearing pointed hats and women by attaching little bells to their dresses.

In 1867 a constitutional enactment from Vienna proclaimed full freedom of religion to the Jews, and they moved into a variety of professions. In the 1880s, the great Hungarian-born Zionist leader Theodor Herzl spent a year in Salzburg as a practising lawyer. As for the music festival, it was rich in Jewish representation – founders, performers and audiences. But post-World War I disillusionment once again made this group less welcome, and World War II brought the ultimate nadir. Only ten of Salzburg's Jewish residents escaped Nazi extermination.

World War II came late to Salzburg. The city, which remarkably had not had a conflict fought upon its soil since the fifth century barbarian invasions, was during 1944 and 1945 bombed sixteen times. Compared with other European cities, the damage was not overwhelming, but neither was it modest: 744 Allied planes dropping 6,000 bombs, 3180 of the town's 7000 houses damaged and 423 totally destroyed, 14,463 people homeless, 531 civilians killed. The cupola of the Dom, the Loreto Church and Mirabell Palace suffered extensive damage.

By the time of the last bombing an Allied victory was not far off. Originally, United States Commander in Europe General Dwight D. Eisenhower had intended that General George Patton advance on Salzburg, but in April 1945, fearing a mountain redoubt at Berchtesgaden, he decided to send the 7th U.S. Army under General Alexander Patch. The expected German resistance did not occur, however, and Salzburg surrendered May 4, five days after Hitler's suicide.

There is some question about how close Salzburg was to being destroyed by the Americans. Some believe that had the S.S. continued to resist, the damage would have been devastating; however, they did not. Evidently, as reported in the book *Salzburg Chronik,* an adamant German general named von Bork issued the order from St. Gilgen that "Salzburg must be defended to the very last." The man to whom he sent the command, one *Oberst* ("Colonel") Lepperdinger, refused to obey because he saw the town was doomed to defeat, and with the Führer already dead, he felt no obligation to follow von Bork's orders. A local historian, Ilse Lackerbauer, has done research indicating that, in any case, the Americans were not planning to shell Salzburg, for negotiations already taking place with the German high command were expected to lead to a peaceful occupation.

Shortly thereafter, the war ended. By June, Patch's troops had departed and others, the 42nd Rainbow Division of World War I fame, had come to Land Salzburg and Upper Austria under Major General Harry J. Collins. The citizens were glad to have the war over with. Hitler's *Anschluss* had amounted to the rape of Austria, bringing only death, destruction and disillusionment. They were glad also to have Americans here instead of the Russians, for they wanted no part of Communism; besides, the U.S. troops had money to buy local goods which, in turn, would help restore the economy to health.

Relations between the two peoples proved during the ten years of the occupation to be very good, an impressive achievement on both sides, given the circumstances. There were, of course, tense times – and tasteless moments. One of the latter occurred toward the end of the occupation when the Americans, ready to depart town, decided to leave a keepsake in the form of a huge rainbow painted over Salzburg's beloved fortress – in permanent, glossy color, no less. The designated artist refused to take on the job, after which a historian in the army became involved and found that U.S. military regulations forbade the changing of historic monuments.

That the occupation was, on the whole, sensitively handled, was due largely to the man at the head. Known as "Hollywood Harry" for his typically American good looks, Major General Collins spoke no German but had married a Salzburg girl (herself a legal advisor to the occupying forces) and developed an unusual rapport with the war-torn city to which he had been assigned.

Collins remained in Salzburg for three years, supervising an ambitious recovery program. His job was not an easy one: the guarding of more than 380,000 prisoners of war and the subsequent discharge and rehabilitation of a number of them, responsibility for one-half million Displaced Persons (including special care for thousands of Jewish refugees) and international and border security. Food, fuel, winterized housing, health care – these were urgent concerns. Collins also organized the return of millions of dollars worth of stolen art treasures to Allied countries. Working closely with local groups, he helped to reestablish democratic institutions such as civil law courts and free elections, to revitalize commerce, transportation and agriculture, to return expropriated church property and transfer German war industries to peaceful production under Austrian direction. Interested in his own troops' education, he began a program whereby they could study and obtain degrees.

While in Salzburg, Harry Collins collected a wealth of scrolls, gifts, honors and titles, the most precious to him being honorary citizenship in the town. He was especially close to the children, bringing them an endless supply of chocolates and piling them up in his jeep for rides. Collins held Christmas parties for 160,000 boys and girls and organized and directed four youth centers and 45 summer camps which enrolled a total of 12,000 youngsters. When he left Salzburg, the children prepared a "before" and "after" book with drawings showing their emaciated appearance in 1945 and their renewed health three years later.

After being recalled to the U.S., Collins was made military attaché to Russia. But he never forgot Salzburg. In fact, he expressed the desire to be buried there. When, in 1963, he suffered a stroke and died while on a special mission to France and Germany, Mrs. Collins called Salzburg's archbishop: "Your Eminence, may I have a grave?" Harry Collins was given a high requiem mass at St. Peter's on a day of pouring rain, after which he was buried in a place of honor before the ancient Margaret Chapel.

Austria's remarkable recovery from the ravages of war is still referred to as the "Austrian miracle," a tribute to the ability of that nation to bounce back from disaster and get on with the business of life. By 1955, with the signing of the Austrian state treaty declaring neutrality and ending foreign occupation, it was well on its way to a financial boom.

In Salzburg, the festival, which had been reinstated during the occupation under the patronage of the U.S. Army, once again began to atract international audiences. Accompanying the musical rebirth was an ambitious tourist campaign under the direction of Dr. Heinz Rennau, who, assisted by a small but energetic staff, was selling Salzburg to the world. With gigantic power plants installed on the Hohen Tauern range along with ski and chair lifts, the area's winter sports could be exploited. By 1965 the super highway connecting Salzburg with Vienna was completed, a further aid to easy travel. Today, one-fourth of Salzburg's income derives from tourism and the rest from trade and specialized small industry, ranging from radios to beer. According to a newspaper report in "The Guardian," the town's beauty, music and ancillary service industries earn for it between $ 400 million and $ 600 million a year.

Politically, Salzburg is headed by a mayor, vice mayor and coalition government, the biggest party on the local council now being socialist – rather a surprise in view of the city's traditional conservatism. According to Austria's constitution, the *Länder*, or provinces, have more power than the towns. At present the conservative People's Party under the *Landeshauptmann* ("Provincial Governor"), Wilfried Haslauer, is in office in Land Salzburg. This is the strongest economic state in the nation, with a per capita income higher than anywhere else except Vienna, Still, it is not easy for the average citizen to live here, for prices – aimed at the affluent tourist – are inflated. Indeed, foreigners have bought up so much of the precious land that what little remains is too costly for many natives. A law now makes foreign purchase of property in Land Salzburg next to impossible.

Among the visitors, neighboring Germany is particularly well represented. Relations between the two peoples are not always easy. There is a tendency on the part of Salzburgers – indeed, of all Austrians – to compare German stiffness, stuffyness, preciseness and humorlessness with their own casual, easy-going, fun-loving attitude, their ability to compromise, their *Gemütlichkeit* (a word impossible to translate but meaning roughly all of these things). No doubt such feelings derive from the historic rivalry of the Habsburg years, a rivalry embittered by the legacy of Hitler. At the same time Austria is proud of the cultural heritage that it shares with Germany. What the country has now that it never had before is a clear sense of nationhood.

The signs of World War II are barely visible now in Salzburg. One must know what to look for: bronze plaques affixed to buildings, landmarks rebuilt, a stark photograph in a church of the city bombed. But more important than the visible is knowledge: a clear recognition of Nazism which, if boldly confronted, will help prevent history's worst holocaust from happening again.

Now and then one encounters in Salzburg a tendency to white-wash it all – the attitude that this is a period of history best forgotten. Most know better.

CHAPTER FOUR
OF CASTLES AND PALACES

No old European town worth its salt is without a few castles and palaces. Salzburg, having become rich from salt, can boast many *Schlösser* – over 20, in fact. Of these we shall discuss the six most famous. They are surprisingly dissimilar both in architecture and purpose, and together they tell us a good deal about Salzburg's past and present. All but two of them (Klesheim and Leopoldskron) are open to the public.

Perched 394 feet above the river Salzach on a ledge of dolomite rock is one of the largest and best preserved medieval fortresses in the world: Festung ("Fortress") Hohensalzburg. As the chief landmark not only of the city but of all Land Salzburg, the massive stone creation can be seen from a great distance, thanks to its size and elevation. The hill on which it stands, the Festungsberg, is separated from the adjacent Mönchsberg by a narrow cleft known as the Scharte. Supported by tremendous walls, Hohensalzburg is composed of a ring of buildings enclosing two extensive courtyards. Its workmen were the weary and sometimes rebellious citizens (initially prisoners) who hauled the building materials up the steep incline on foot and with the help of horses and oxen.

The Festung was created to protect Salzburg's powerful prince archbishops from both external and home-grown enemies. Enlarged and changed over many centuries, it managed to maintain its harmony and compactness, at the same time responding to advances in military science (for instance, when the invention of gunpowder made square turrets obsolete, round towers were introduced). Hohensalzburg served its purpose well, being virtually impregnable for more than 700 years. An awesome sight even today, the fortress must have sobered many a medieval citizen of Salzburg who looked up at its weapon-filled bastions. And any trouble-maker foolish enough to risk the climb found broken glass strewn plentifully about, with nary a tree for hiding.

We have spoken of Archbishop Gebhard who began the erection of Hohensalzburg in 1077, just before the First Crusade. A faithful servant of the pope, he was in considerable danger during the investiture controversy between emperor and pope, since many powerful overlords of Germany were on the emperor's side. Hohensalzburg was one of three castles built by Gebhard for protection against these overlords.

51

His successors, one after another, added to the fortress, the contributions of the ruthless Leonhard von Keutschach being among the most extensive. Fearing – with good reason – his fellow citizens, Leonhard moved here from town into specially built and princely quarters. His successor Matthäus Lang took refuge in the Festung during the Peasant's Rebellion, awaiting rescue by the Prince of Bavaria. Among Lang's contributions was a heavy tower bristling with cannons which overlooked the town; this the archbishop mockingly referred to as his *Bürgermeister* ("Master of the Burghers"). Almost a century later along came Wolf Dietrich who was more interested in building churches than stocking arsenals; he had the ill fortune to end his days in Hohensalzburg as prisoner. The later additions by Paris Lodron were significant in helping the town remain safe during the Thirty Years War, and the last notable defense measure was a bastion erected by Max Gondolf von Kuenburg. With the secularization of Salzburg in 1803 the fortress, then finally outdated, was given over to Napoleon's men. From then on Hohensalzburg, like Salzburg itself, passed from one master to another. In the 1860s it ceased to be considered a military fortress and was opened to the public with a railway installed for easy access.

Among the areas of visitor interest are the State Apartments on the fourth floor of the Inner Castle, built for Leonhard von Keutschach at the beginning of the 16th century. These constitute one of the finest examples of late Gothic secular architecture in Central Europe. Of particular note are the delicate scroll work upon the doors and the richly gilded and carved walls. In these apartments, much restored through the years, various archbishops slept, dined, passed judgments on sinners, held courts of law and hid in time of peril and war from foreign invaders and their own subjects.

The most remarkable room of the State Apartments is the Goldene Stube ("Golden Chamber") which contains a stove, nearly 14 feet high, a masterpiece of the medieval potter's art. Square in shape at its base and octagonal above, the stove stands on five carved lions. It is covered with unusually thin tiles, each one different; depicted upon them are flowers, fruits, scenes from church history, saints and rulers. Once attributed to a Nüremberg workshop, the stove was later found to be the creation of an unknown local master from Hallein. A portrait on one of the tiles features a curly haired fellow attired in a yellow doublet; there is talk, but no real proof, that he is the artist. The Golden Chamber also has a wealth of woodcarving, of mystic and supernatural significance.

The Goldener Saal ("Golden Hall") is a dramatic room, its blue ceiling studded with gold like a starry sky; a frieze just below is decorated with a variety of coats-of-arms: Empire, Austrian provinces, bishops, noble families, etc. Supporting the ceiling by the north wall are four massive pillars of red Adnet marble with twisted stems; one of them is said to have been damaged by a cannon ball when the fortress was besieged during the Peasants' Rebellion.*

Along the ramparts, the visitor to Hohensalzburg reaches the so-called Salzburg Stier ("Bull"), a great, hand-driven barrel organ dating from 1502 – also the idea of our friend Leonhard. With over 200 tin pipes operated by a wind mechanism, the organ gained its nickname from the loud chords played at the start and finish of the chorale – chords that decidedly recall the lowing of a bull. This similarity was intentional: Leonhard had the organ built so as to remind the disgruntled citizens below that he was still master. The "Bull" plays today as it has for centuries, at 7 a.m. and 11 a.m. and 6 p.m. Only one chorale sounded during Leonhard's time, but later less forbidding works were written for it by musicians attached to the court, such as Leopold Mozart and Michael Haydn.

Those interested in further mementos of the unsavory Leonhard von Keutschach can find a memorial to the gentleman outside the fortress's St. George's Chapel, built in 1501; this is in the form of a great relief in red marble, attributed to Hans Valkenauer, which depicts Leonhard standing piously in full pontificals with his hand raised in blessing between two deacons.

Among the biggest tourist attractions at Hohensalzburg are the torture chambers and dungeons. Torture was made legal during the 16th century reign of King Charles V and it was not abolished until the second half of the 18th century. So during that period Salzburg's archbishops could, if they wished, invent all kinds of ways to torment the populace. Special instruments in Hohensalzburg were used to extract confessions and execute sentences. Prisoners might be chained to walls with hand and foot fetters, burned, guillotined, publicly exhibited, or exposed to red-hot stoves and thrown into the dungeons deep below. The wheel was the most notorious in-

---

* Bauer gives us one of his vivid descriptions: "The Goldener Saal was originally designed with only three walls; the fourth side was open to the city below, justice being dispensed in a sort of open loggia. The blue roof studded with gold dovetailed into the blue sky, and the four twisted pillars of Untersberg marble were like stalagmites sprouting from the rock."

strument of death. Those punished included heretics, Protestants and delinquent taxpayers (the latter were starved until they produced the money). Max Gandolf von Kuenberg specialized in hunting witches and sorcerers. These are but a few of the Festung highlights. One can wander for hours discovering something new: round towers, a maze of courtyards, ancient lime trees, piles of cannon balls, huge bread ovens built into the wall. A museum is devoted to Gothic and Renaissance religious sculpture and painting. For refreshments and a rest there is a scenically located café-restaurant. The funicular runs up and down the mountain from Festungsgasse during warmer months, but climbing the lovely wooded road with the help of steps and rails enables one to have a better understanding of this historic example of man's ability at self-protection.

For those whose time is limited a guided tour is useful, so long as one does not treat all the information presented as fact. The so-called "Hangman's House," for instance, which dates from the 16th century and stands below the fortress in a large meadow, was almost certainly never the home of the executioner of Salzburg; historians posit that it did serve as lodgings for the supervisor of the fields (or "guardian of the cabbage," as he was called) for St. Peter's Monastery.

Among Salzburg's more embarrassing memories is the near demolition of the Hohensalzburg. Back in the mid 19th century when it became necessary for the river Salzach to be regulated so as to prevent flooding, it occurred to some practical-minded citizens that the unused Festung would provide a lot of stones for such a purpose. In addition, they argued, just think of all the nice land that would be available for building a hotel once the castle had been razed. Fortunately, good sense won and the Festung was allowed to remain standing, just as the river was allowed to retain its curve.

Later generations have realized how precious a possession is their fortress. Today Hohensalzburg is visited by more than one million people annually. On the occasion of its 900th birthday in summer 1977 the town organized a week-long celebration. There were lectures, photography exhibits, puppet shows, special masses, and a gala procession with musical bands, riflemen and folklore groups in traditional costume from as far as the South Tyrol and Bavaria. Capping the week's events was a spectacular display of fireworks from the Festung, with great globes and fans and shooting stars in brilliant colors lighting the night sky.

Even more significant is that the fortress continues to be a living, growing place – not just a museum. One of the first people to realize its great potential was Austrian painter, lithographer and poet Oskar Kokoschka who in 1953 first used the Festung as the scene for an International Summer Academy where various fine arts were taught. In this he worked closely with local art gallery owner Friedrich Welz. The unifying principle was an attempt to help students rediscover and refine their sense of vision and through this to open their eyes to what truly is art: a "School of Vision." The course became a huge success. Though Kokoschka is no longer alive (he died in February 1980),the Academy still bears his strong imprint. Each summer students from over 30 nations work here and in other historic buildings, taught by distinguished artists in such fields as architecture, stage design, sculpture, etching, lithography, photography, calligraphy and goldsmithery. In Kokoschka's own words, "... the International Academy in Salzburg... considers it the task of the citizens of the world to see the world as the living heritage of the past, which surrounds us during life and which at the same time is ever and ever again newly born in every person when he experiences his or her creative moment." He could not have chosen a more appropriate setting than Hohensalzburg.

To comprehend the power of Salzburg's ruling archbishops, one must see the Residenz (Residence), their onetime official home. Located in the Old Town on a square of the same name – Paumgartner calls this square "the ceremonial anteroom of temporal majesty in this land which, though open to the world, knew how to keep aloof when necessary" – the Residenz is an imposing arrangement of buildings around three courtyards. In admiring it, one almost forgets the less attractive circumstances of its origin: the ripping out of the cemetery and scores of residents' homes by Wolf Dietrich. Nor can we fully picture today how it must have looked in its heyday, say, in Paris Lodron's time, with carriages in procession, couriers and bodyguards, mounted arquebusiers and court musicians in colorful uniforms, peasant weddings and animal baitings.*
The Salzburg bishops held court in this same location from the 12th century in a rambling complex of buildings, mostly medieval in style and with gable roofs. Wolf Dietrich, dreaming of Renaissance

---

* It was considered an amusing entertainment to pile together beasts of every description and watch them kill each other. If events weren't lively enough, a donkey with a pickled herring tied to his tail might be used to titillate the other animals.

Rome, wanted to get rid of the stuffy, cramped feeling, the old-fashioned look. In 1590 he began the construction of the New Building (Neugebäude) on the east side of the square. Bearing his family's coat-of-arms, its ceilings richly decorated with carved wood and colored stucco work, this edifice was to serve as temporary quarters for him and eventually for the housing of visiting potentates. Meanwhile he began to enlarge and modernize the old Bishop's Court opposite; such amounted almost to full demolition, with only the main walls left standing.

It took a good half century to complete the building that is today's Residenz, Markus Sittikus and Paris Lodron taking over the work left unfinished by Wolf Dietrich. So spacious was the result that by the time of the Cathedral's consecration in 1628, 13 princes and their entourages were able to stay here in comfort without imposing on the archbishop's privacy. Possessed of a simple harmony, the Renaissance-style building has 180 rooms. Its imposing staircase was designed so as to be ascended by riders on horseback. The doorway was probably the work of Italian-born Johann Lukas von Hildebrandt, leading architect rival to Fischer von Erlach and creator of Vienna's two Belvedere palaces. An interesting feature is the placement of the Residenz in relation to Salzburg's leading places of worship: the Cathedral, St. Peter's and the Franciscan Church; without so much as going outdoors the archbishop could enter any of these churches from his palatial home.

The second-floor State Rooms of the Residenz are open for tours and are well worth a visit. Here are portraits of the archbishops, their vestments and private altars, giving an intimate look into the tastes and appearance of the inhabitants. The largest room of the palace is the Carabinierisaal where the archbishop's bodyguards kept watch day and night. The ceiling paintings here, mythological in subject, are by Johann Michael Rottmayr, who was responsible for most of the important frescoes in the Residenz; others are by Martin Altomonte. Rottmayr, born in 1654 at nearby Laufen-on-the-Salzach (then part of the archbishopric) studied in Venice where he developed a gift for almost impressionistic lighting effects combined with a sensual use of color, especially in depicting garments. He was the artist most favored as partner by Fischer von Erlach, and he specialized in the designs (historical, religious and mythological) that filled the huge surfaces and cupolas of churches and palaces. Rottmayr did a good deal of other work in Salzburg but scored his biggest successes in Vienna where he was raised to the nobility. One can see in the frescoes of the Residenz a style characteristic of the Austrian baroque: healthy, strong, honest and spontaneous, without empty elegance.

Also of note is the Conference Room which has a beautiful stove of the Louis XVI period; here Mozart took part in court concerts. Most elaborately furnished is the Audience Room which, in addition to works by Rottmayr, has valuable Gobelins tapestries showing scenes from Roman history and thought to be from 16th century Brussels; its floor is the original one of parquet and there are Venetian candelabras and finely tapestried 18th century furniture. In the Picture Gallery is a stove of different kinds of colored marble – a superb example of Salzburg craftsmanship. Portraits of all the Habsburg emperors from the 13th to 18th centuries hang in the Kaisersaal.

A fine art gallery of European painting from the 16th to 20th century is located on the third floor of the Residenz. Along with works by such titans as Rembrandt, Rubens and Titian, one finds paintings of local interest, especially those by Hans Makart. Makart, for whom a town square and bridge are named, was a lively character as much remembered today for his flamboyant life as for his art. Born in Salzburg in 1840, the son of an inspector at Mirabell Palace, he became a favorite of the Emperor Franz Joseph who furnished a villa for him in Vienna; this developed into a mecca for dilettantes, tourists and society ladies. Makart boasted that some of the latter had posed for him in the nude, a bold claim in those days but one that many of the ladies were happy to verify. Makart attracted attention also for his vast, tapestry-like historical paintings. He was a man of the theater, being called upon to supervise a five-hour pageant featuring the music of Wagner to celebrate the 25th wedding anniversary of the Emperor and his Elisabeth; at the event Makart appeared in black silk on a white horse, bowing to the applause of a crowd that numbered one million. When he died of paralysis caused by syphilis, he was given the most elaborate funeral ever accorded in Vienna to a non-noble. Salzburg remains loyal to its talented if wayward son, but critics tend to be harsh; one of them, William M. Johnston, wrote, "Feted to satiety, he produced paintings so deficient in basic temperament that however he may have excelled at reviving the past, he bequeathed little for posterity to admire."

The Residenz has been relatively quiet since the secularization of Salzburg, when many of its precious possessions vanished, never to return. Still, renovations have continued to the present century, and the building remains in active – if not princely – use. Banquets seating up to 500 are held, and concerts, mostly featuring works by Mozart,are given in several of the rooms and in the courtyard. Every spring an antique show brings dealers from all over Austria to sell their prize possessions at top prices. A few offices are housed in the palace including that of the vice-chancellor of Salzburg's university.

The New Building, which now is home to the general post office and the offices of the provincial government, has a particularly charming feature: the Glockenspiel, located in the tower. This was the addition of the Archbishop Johann Ernst von Thun, rich from his trading activities in the Dutch East India Company. Thun bought the carillon from a famous Antwerp bell founder in 1695 (it had been cast for a church that was destroyed by fire). A year later the mechanism was transported to Salzburg via three boxes on two horses. Unfortunately, parts were missing and an experienced Dutch mechanic couldn't be found who was willing to take on the job; one lay brother refused to set out on the trip, declaring that he was sick and unwilling to die in Salzburg where there would be no Dutch-speaking confessor. So finally, after much delay, a local watchmaker, Jeremias Sauter, began the delicate work. Carillons being new to Salzburg, the resultant work was not too precise.

For centuries the carillon was run by hand, but now it is powered by electro-mechanical means, being automatically set by the four clocks in the tower; different melodies are adjusted on the barrel and changed each month. It's worth a climb up the winding eight flights of stairs for a tour and to watch the carillon in motion. From directly above the mechanism the clanging of its giant bells (the largest weighs 839 pounds) is deafening. Slightly and delightfully out of tune and unbalanced in rhythm as a result of its faulty installation, the carillon renders melodies by Mozart, hymns and carols – truly one of Salzburg's most characteristic voices.

Fountains, as any visitor to Salzburg will discover, are many and imaginative, and the one in the center of the Residenzplatz is among the most beautiful and largest north of the Alps. A gracefully Italian counterpart to the monumentality of the Residenz, it was built under the reign of Archbishop Guidobald Count of Thun, probably by Tommaso di Garona. Made of marble from the Untersberg, the intricate Renaissance-style work is 50 feet high. Its basin represents a flower with eight petals; upon it is sculpted Thun's coat-of-arms. In the basin, four sea horses spout jets of water, and a structure of

58

rocks holds three naked men who carry a flat water bowl. Three dolphins reside in the bowl; their tails, turned upwards and twisted, hold another smaller, fluted bowl carrying the Triton, sea demigod. He, in turn, throws water upwards out of a shell which he holds with both hands to his mouth. The water flows over the brim of the full bowl into the wide basin, forming a mirror of blue-green water which reflects the images of man and beast.

Walking along the shop-filled and heavily trafficked street Schwarzstrasse in the heart of the New Town, one comes unexpectedly upon a haven of verdant green: the formal park and gardens of Schloss Mirabell ("Mirabell Palace"). Here residents and visitors doze in the sun, take photos among the statuary, buy bouquets of dried flowers from vendors. Here, in summer, they gaze at the roses and attend free outdoor band concerts and, at Easter, choose *en famille* from a large variety of live bunny rabbits. In the morning, when it is quiet, music-lovers listen to strains of song from the neighboring Mozarteum; in the evening weary walkers sit quietly, admiring the facade of the Mirabell Palace, shrimp-colored in the fading sun. Sometimes a flock of nuns glides by, their black habits in stark contrast to the brilliant floral carpet.

Mirabell was quite a different place when first built by Wolf Dietrich in 1606 for his lifelong companion Salome. The area at that time, composed of uninhabited fields, was outside the town walls. Altenau, a quadrangular building with tower, was a splendid country seat for the beauteous lady but, as we have seen, her tenure there ended tragically with the imprisonment of her princely lover. Markus Sittikus, who took over the archbishopric and, with it, Altenau, wanted to draw a veil over his predecessor's scandalous liaison and so had it remodeled and renamed Mirabell; he then took pains to avoid it. Not so his successor Paris Lodron, who had bastions built around it, incorporated it into the city and hosted gala events within its walls.

Through the centuries the Schloss has undergone many extensive alterations. Nothing remains of the original and, because of the disastrous town fire in 1818, not much is left of the work by architect Hildebrandt, whose baroque rendering under Archbishop Franz Anton von Harrach constituted Mirabell's finest hour. Fortunately undamaged was a supreme example of Hildebrandt's talent: the upstairs Marble Room, used today as civil wedding chamber* and, softly candlelit, as the setting for year-round chamber music concerts. Its floor is of marble in strongly contrasting colors, and the walls are of stucco marble with elegant gilt scroll work. During the fire only the ceiling, which contained a Rottmayr fresco, was destroyed.

The other remnant of the Hildebrandt period is the main staircase sculpted by Georg Rafael Donner, a native of Lower Austria. Staircases of important buildings afforded the baroque artist an ideal opportunity for ingenious and exuberant ornamentation. Donner produced an especially charming example of this highly specialized art in Mirabell. This is a light-hearted creation: an array of white marble *putti* (cherubs) with round bodies, short legs and children's faces, riding upon the crests of waves of the lavishly decorated baluster. They climb, lie, slide and struggle in turbulent motion, their gestures reflecting all manner of emotion, from puzzlement to mock despair. (Since the staircase leads directly to the Marble Room, attendees at weddings there have interpreted these cherubic gestures accordingly.) In the niches of the stairwell are sculpted mythological figures. One, the porous, coarse-grained Paris in loin cloth and carrying a flute, was the work of Donner himself; assistants from his workshop did the other figures according to his models.

A final rebuilding of Schloss Mirabell after the fire, according to plans by Peter von Nobile, has given the structure its present unassuming and mundane neo-classical appearance. As a municipal office it is seat of the mayor of Salzburg; it also houses a museum devoted to baroque art.

The gardens surrounding Schloss Mirabell were laid out in Wolf Dietrich's day, expanded by Markus Sittikus and reorganized under Count Johann Ernst Thun. Thun hired architect Fischer von Erlach to redesign the gardens in a genuinely baroque fashion that would assure their harmony vis à vis the town's leading buildings (Fortress, Cathedral and Residence), all of which can be seen from this spot.

---

* To be legally married in present-day Austria, one must take part in a civil ceremony at a government office such as Mirabell. A religious ceremony is optional. Hence to be married in the eyes of both church and state, the couple will have two ceremonies. Mirabell's big wedding day is Saturday morning. So popular is the Marble Room that foreigners often come here to be wed, lured by the romantic mode of transportation advertised by the tourist office (a coach and six) as well as by the beauty of Mirabell.

Mirabell's statuary is abundant but unequal in quality, numerous pieces having been moved here from other locations. The center of the garden is dominated by four large groups representing the four elements by a Padua-born resident of Salzburg, Ottavio Mosto. A bronze version of the male horse Pegasus by Caspar Gras (1661) of Innsbruck stands in front of the southern facade in the center of a circular water basin. Oldtime Salzburgers chuckle when they remember that Gras' Pegasus was "castrated" back in the 1930s thanks to the efforts of a high-born and influential lady who objected to the distinctive marks of its sex. (This story is one of many in the delightful, if poorly translated, book *All About Salzburg*, edited by Kaut.)

Another typically baroque feature of the park is its Dwarf Garden, populated by numerous squat marble figures – some hunchbacks, others with goitres. Dwarves were employed in the court of Archbishop Franz Anton von Harrach; it was he who had the stone figures erected for a theater, later closed. Averaging 4'3" in height, the humorous figures represent popular Salzburg citizens of that time and stock comic characters. Also in the park is the so-called Hedge Theater, which probably was modeled on the Tuilleries Gardens in Paris. It was used for summer performances as early as 1717; seats were long benches overgrown with grass.

As frivolous in its purpose as the fortress was serious is Schloss Hellbrunn (meaning "Palace Clear Fountain"), creation of that practical-joking archbishop, Markus Sittikus. While it was being built, Wolf Dietrich lay awaiting death in Hohensalzburg.

Designed in the manner of northern Italian and Roman villas* by the Cathedral architect Santino Solari, Hellbrunn was intended for the lighter side of life: feasting and imbibing, hunting, promenading, music- and love-making. Tradition has it that Sittikus built the palace for Belgian-born Madame de Mabon, wife of his guards captain. Commissioned shortly after Sittikus came to power in 1612, Hellbrunn was novel in style for Salzburg and had a strong influence on later secular architecture. It is located a few miles to the south of the city.

Hellbrunn's possessions – or, rather, what little remains of the original sumptuous furnishings – are a hodgepodge of the local and imported, artistic and bizarre. One sees paintings of an eight-legged

* Bauer refers to Hellbrunn as "an example of a typical Salzburg obsession that refuses to recognize that Salzburg is not in Italy."

horse and other freak animals, Chinese wallpaper, a delicately ornamented pottery stove, a multicolored mosaic floor of Salzburg marble, ingeniously contrived perspective views by a Florentine monk of streets and buildings against a background of the Uffizi Palace in Florence and St. Mark's Cathedral in Venice. One portrait shows the archbishop himself: grand and lordlike, with a narrow face, high forehead and thick black beard; serving as backdrop is the half finished Dom, and in one hand Sittikus holds a portrait of Hellbrunn.

The personality of Sittikus is even more vividly revealed in the palace grounds. He was a man fascinated by water and the new science of hydraulics, as demonstrated by the wetter side of Hellbrunn: its charming Wasserspiele (literally "water games"), whose inspiration was also Italian. The "Roman Theater," for instance, features a long stone dinner table with benches for guests. Running down the middle of the table is a trough in which wine was cooled. When the archbishop felt like sobering up his dinner company, he would signal a servant to turn on a hidden tap, causing jets of ice-cold water to rise up from holes in the seats of the benches onto the backsides of the startled diners. Etiquette demanded that none rise before the archbishop did so; his own seat remaining bone dry, Sittikus naturally stayed seated.

A series of highly imaginative grottos further carries out the water theme. One, in honor of Neptune, the bearded water god, is decorated in stone mosaic and encrusted with shells. At Neptune's feet are two sea horses and a hilarious Groucho Marx kind of face with fat eyebrows and huge ears. Natives call him "Big Mouth," an appropriate name, for when his lower jaw fills with water his mouth opens, the long red tongue sticks out and the eyes roll. (Some say this was the archbishop's response to those who criticized the extravagance and levity of Hellbrunn.)

A more romantic spot is the Birdsong Grotto, decorated like a forest cave and filled with melodious sounds of birds; you will look in vain for live feathered creatures, for the singing is mechanically produced by water pressure. In contrast, the Orpheus Grotto is entirely covered in volcanic rock. It contains statues of Orpheus and Euridice in the Underworld; supposedly the Euridice is a likeness of Madame de Mabon and the portrait around her neck that of Sittikus. There is no end to the fun. A bishop's crown jumps up from its base through water pressure, stone turtles spit water into each other's mouths, jets of water balance balls high in the air and fan out from the antlers of stags. As if that weren't enough, no matter where visitors go to hide, water will unexpectedly drench them – from above, below, behind, from all sides. (Hence a raincoat is sorely needed in Hellbrunn, whatever the weather.) This prank is carried out by the castle's tour guides who have lots of fun in the process and, like Sittikus, always manage to remain dry themselves.

Among the more serious features of the Schloss is its Steintheater "stone theater" on the slope of Hellbrunn Mountain, which reflected Markus Sittikus' strong interest in music and drama. In creating this outdoor theater he set a precedent for Salzburg's musical future; here, in 1617, an opera was staged for the first time on German soil: *Santa Christina*. Three centuries later this very spot was chosen, then discarded, as the focal point for Salzburg's summer festival. However, the theater has been renovated and once again is used for operatic performances.

The Steintheater, from where the stone to build Hellbrunn itself was probably quarried, is a stark and dramatic setting, utilizing a natural cave in the rocks as the stage. Seated in the audience area at the bottom of a deep hollow, one is transported back to Sittikus' day. (Interestingly, even he was a relative latecomer to these parts, for Hellbrunn Hill, along with Rainberg, was witness to Salzburg's earliest human habitation during the Stone Age.)

On the other side of the same mountain is located the Monatschlössl ("Little Palace built in a month"), a charming, rustic dwelling that was created by Solari for Markus Sittikus upon the suggestion of visiting royalty – probably the Archduke Maximilian who was in the area taking the cure. Sittikus, anxious to show Maximilian how quickly his idea was acted upon, made sure it was complete within the month; hence its name. Now the building houses a small but intriguing museum of regional folklore, with hand-painted peasant furniture, Alpine horns, Krampus figures*, etc.

A later addition to Hellbrunn, one in keeping with its light spirit, is the mechanical theater. Commissioned in 1750 by Archbishop Andreas Jakobus von Dietrichstein, it was mainly carved by the salt miner Lorenz Rosenegger of Dürrnberg, who spent some four years on this intricate task. Composed of over 100 moving parts – all of them powered by (what else?) water, the scene is of busy town life during the Middle Ages. Gypsies dance with a tame bear, guards

* See chapter 9.

march, a butcher kills a calf, and a street band performs; over all this din an organ chorale written by Leopold Mozart's teacher booms forth.

When the movement stops and quiet is restored, there's a final touch. Knowing visitors all shout *"Wasser!"* and sure enough, within seconds the audience is sprayed again. The spirit of that mischievous archbishop Markus Sittikus must be lingering nearby, laughing heartily.

Long before Schloss Hellbrunn was built, there was a deer park in the area of Hellbrunn Mountain. Since 1961 a modern and highly scientific zoological garden has been located here, utilizing the natural mountain backdrop and with many of the animals roaming free (the vultures sometimes fly as far as 30 miles away, returning every day). One sees brilliantly colored parrots, doves, peacocks strutting proudly in their elegant attire, silver pheasants with red foreheads and long black heads of hair, wild boars, reindeer, monkeys, buffaloes, porcupines, mountain goats, bears. For the weary – and many are at the end of a day at Hellbrunn – there is a welcome, electrically run foot massage.

Special summer evening events at Hellbrunn combine tours of the grounds and palace with performances of the kind of music Sittikus would have heard. A wine cellar created by a later archbishop offers refreshment by candlelight.

All the year round, tour buses line up across the lake from Salzburg's Schloss Leopoldskron, and visitors jump out cameras in hand to record one of Austria's most idyllic scenes. The splendor is both man- and nature-made: shimmering water inhabited by proud white swans and ringed at the far edge with water lilies, formal gardens which front onto the three-story rococo palace. Leopoldskron is a building of exquisite and symmetrical grace; though noble in appearance it is light-hearted, though regal, inviting. Behind, in somber contrast, massive Hohensalzburg broods, and to the south of the lake, stretching its long back toward Bavaria, there rises the Untersberg, ever different: cloaked in mist or wearing an ermine mantle or with every ridge etched clearly in the sunlight.

Built in 1736, Leopoldskron is an Austrian national monument; as such it is pictured on the one thousand Schilling note. The edifice owes its existence to the choleric, hermit-like archbishop Leopold Firmian, remembered for his expulsion of the Protestants from Salzburg. The erection of Leopoldskron – "The Crown of Leopold" – was an attempt by the archbishop to enhance his family's declining social standing. It turned out to be a crown befitting any monarch. The architect was a Scottish Benedictine, P. Bernard Stuart, who also was a mathematician, astrologer and clockmaker. The wall and ceiling stucco work (considered to be among the finest examples of this art in Europe) as well as the marble staircase, were the creation of his assistant, the Austrian Johann Kleber. Like many collaborations, the behind-the-scenes story of Leopoldskron is not so pretty as the structure itself; Kleber sued Stuart, claiming that Leopoldskron's design was his own and that he'd been cheated. As a result, Stuart fell into disgrace and left the country. But it appears quite clear today from construction plans that Kleber had done the cheating and that the architect was, indeed, Stuart.

Whoever did what, the new family seat was so beloved by Leopold Firmian that upon his death in 1744 his heart was buried in its chapel floor, while his body, as was customary, went to the Cathedral. Schloss Leopoldskron passed to Leopold's nephew Laktanz, a man much interested in art, subsequently to his son, and then to a motley variety of owners. These included an ex-king of Bavaria whose wife, a practising Protestant – in fitting, if belated, rejoinder to Firmian – held services in the chapel, a pair of waiters who wanted to turn the building into a hotel with mud baths, and a shooting gallery proprietor who took out everything he could, including works of art and even the parquet floors.

Luckily for Leopoldskron, in 1917 along came Max Reinhardt, the Austrian stage director who was about to found the summer festival in Salzburg with a handful of other brilliant men. Reinhardt bought the palace, the surrounding estate and the lake. Theatrical to the core, he used the body of water to transport his guests back and forth via gondola; the banks, naturally, were torch-lit. Often he entertained his *literati* friends with performances in an outdoor theater ringed by trees; Shakespeare's *A Midsummer Night's Dream* starring Reinhardt's actress wife Helene Thimig was a favorite.

The new owner expended money and effort to replace paintings and sculpture taken out by the *Schloss'* former inhabitants; when possible he repurchased Firmian's original possessions. He also made important room additions. One was a library modelled on that of the 18th century monastery library in St. Gallen, Switzerland; with theatrical motifs depicted on the ceiling plaster work, a secret staircase, and fat cherrywood cherubs leaping from the pinnacled shelves, it is a sanctuary as suited to daydreaming as to study.

Another is a glittering "Venetian Room" with wall panels imported from an Italian *palazzo;* when candlelit, the chandelier casts the room in a glow of burnished gold and reflected mirrors.

Reinhardt, a Jew, left Austria with the coming of World War II; meanwhile, no longer the scene of Shakespeare and song, Schloss Leopoldskron became a grim place as Gauleiter reception and meeting headquarters. Miraculously, it escaped serious damage during the many bombings of the town.

After the war, in 1947, there began one of the most exciting chapters in the history of the Schloss – a chapter that continues to this day. Three students at Harvard University, aware that Europe was suffering from intellectual as well as physical starvation, conceived the idea of a summer academic program to be held in Austria. The subject would be American civilization – considered relatively safe in those tense days – and the language English. The session would be conducted, at no remuneration, by some of America's finest professors and attended by Europeans (western and eastern and from both sides of the war) whose higher education and careers had been cut off by the hostilities.

Officially Harvard did not think much of the idea, but the young men persisted, gaining funds, a group of enthusiastic students or "Fellows," a superb faculty including anthropologist Margaret Mead and economist Wassily Leontieff, and – last, but not least – a setting: Schloss Leopoldskron, rented from the heirs of the then deceased Max Reinhardt. With Care packages flown in from Switzerland, ten-pound sacks of flour contributed by participating Americans, and an assortment of sleeping bags, a first session of the Salzburg Seminar in American Studies was held. For the Europeans, many of them crippled in body and spirit, it was an unprecedented joy finally to exchange weapons of war for words of communication.

Today the same Seminar is a pride of American academia. Headquartered in Cambridge, Massachusetts as a non-profit educational institution, with close but not official ties to a now highly receptive Harvard, it offers seven or eight sessions per year, each for two or three weeks, on subjects ranging from post-industrial society to multinational enterprise and contemporary American music. The 9,000 alumni roster reads like a "Who's Who in Europe" and encompasses fields as diverse as architecture, politics and the performing arts. Within the eastern bloc, all nations except Albania send Fellows – a remarkable sign of trust. Teaching, still at no pay, are

American, and, increasingly, European, men and women of note: university presidents and Nobel Laureates, corporation heads and Pulitzer Prize poets, composers and Supreme Court Justices. In recent years representation from the Middle East and the developing world has been growing on both the Faculty and Fellow levels. The Seminar is thus rapidly becoming a truly global institution. Schloss Leopoldskron is now in the peculiar position of being a national monument of Austria but the possession of an American institution; in 1959 it was purchased by the Seminar. Because the building is generally full to the brim with scholars, tours are not feasible. People who live right across the lake may not be aware of the excitement generated within unless they attend a session or are invited to a special event like the gala 30th birthday celebration in summer 1977, when Chancellor of Austria Bruno Kreisky gave the keynote address. (So vital an institution is the Seminar in official Austrian eyes that the government for several years has provided a substantial portion of the annual budget.)

Salzburgers, at least the old-timers, tend to look back nostalgically to the days when their fellow countryman Max Reinhardt owned Schloss Leopoldskron, but many of them are quick to add that Reinhardt himself would have been delighted to see the building's present use. And the lake with its fishing rights has been returned to the citizens. When winter comes and the water freezes over, Firmian's old home becomes a skater's paradise. It is then that the most dramatic view of Leopoldskron can be captured on camera by standing right in the middle of the frozen lake.

Of all Salzburg's *Schlösser,* the one most likely to be heard of by people who never visited the town is Klesheim, for its name crops up with predictable frequency these days on the front pages of newspapers. Politically neutral Austria, being strategically located in the heart of Europe, is ideally suited as a meeting place between world leaders. The nation has no more beautiful city than Salzburg – an added attraction for sophisticated diplomats. Of the many palaces, imposing Klesheim is the one most often chosen; possessing all the amenities a head of state could ask, this fine example of Viennese High Baroque has seen more than its share of formal dinners, press conferences and high-level talks.

On such state visits Salzburg officialdom outdoes itself, setting up meals at picturesque restaurants like the hillside Kobenzl Hotel or the Jagdschloss* at Lake Fuschl, and having the visiting delegation met at the airport by the colorful honor guards known as the Salzburg Riflemen; this company has a toy-soldier appearance with its peaked and plumed military caps and its blue jackets trimmed in braid and piping. Sometimes the welcome is less than festive: on former U. S. President Richard M. Nixon's 1972 visit he was met not only by Chancellor Kreisky and the Riflemen but by 1500 citizens demonstrating against the Vietnam War; among them was Kreisky's own son, Peter.

Speaking of Nixon, at the time of his stay at Klesheim, the White House was particularly obsessed with security and privacy. It so happened that movie producer Gottfried Reinhardt, in order to reach his own residence which lies on Klesheim's grounds, would have to pass directly under the presidential window. Wanting to prevent such an unwanted intrusion, the White House asked that a special bypass road be created for use by Mr. Reinhardt. Egyptian President Anwar-el-Sadat has been a Klesheim guest, too, meeting here in 1975 with American President Gerald R. Ford (it was the famous "trick knee" visit when Ford tripped on the airplane ramp, then told the assembled crowd, "I am sorry I tumbled in"). Sadat also came to Salzburg to walk with leaders of Israel's opposition party as a follow-up to his dramatic 1977 peace mission in Israel.

Klesheim does not maintain such a lofty clientele at all times. It is, in fact, rather an odd mixture of elegance and ordinary business, housing a hotel management school (in the basement), a summer school, a seminar for second and third level diplomats, and a hotel with golf and swimming facilities. Functions of one kind or another are held at Schloss Klesheim approximately 70 days per year – everything from bank functions to automobile shows – with participants paying for use of the facilities. The general public, unfortunately, cannot tour the palace.

Klesheim was commissioned in about 1700 by Archbishop Johann Count Thun, with Fischer von Erlach as architect. Originally known as "Favorita," the Palladian-style villa is located two miles to the northwest of the city proper in a beautiful wooded park and pheasant preserve which ran down to the river Salzach, marking the frontier with Bavaria. Fischer drew up the plans – his first for a sovereign's palace – but didn't finish the construction because he was

---

* once an archbishops' hunting lodge, now a hotel

called to Vienna; court architect Bernard Stuart, creator of Leopoldskron, took over, evolving a toned-down version of Fischer's design. Only partially built during Thun's time, Klesheim was continued by his successor Franz Anton von Harrach and by Harrach's successor Leopold Firmian. Upon the secularization of Salzburg, Klesheim was occupied by the Archduke of the House of Habsburg, brother to Emperor Franz Joseph. After the dissolution of the Empire, it became the property of the province.

During World War II Hitler took over Klesheim. It is not difficult to understand why. Surrounded by a high wall and entered through a forbidding gate, the Schloss is set back far on extensive grounds, the gardens geometrically patterned and precise. Severe, cool, undeniably grand, Klesheim inspires awe – and even fear. Just what the Führer wanted. He had the building extensively restored, and built a private railroad station from here to his nearby Berchtesgaden retreat. Hosting such unsavory figures as Martin Bormann and planning his Thousand Year *Reich,* he intended that Klesheim be the splendid setting from which he would preside over an Allied surrender. With the end of the hostilities – Hitler's Thousand Year *Reich* having crumbled into ruins – Schloss Klesheim was occupied by American troops. At present it is once again the property of the *Land.*

A double ramp sweeps up to Klesheim's colonnaded entrance. On the first floor the large two-storey hall contains a circular gallery from which orchestral groups, invisible from the hall, provide music for special functions. The stucco work is by Paolo de Allio and Diego Francesco Carlone, and there is one fresco: by Julio Quaglio (1709), depicting Noah after the landing of the Ark. (It is located, of all places, in the bathroom of one of the state apartments. So high is the ceiling that a special overhead light had to be installed for easy viewing of the fresco by such illustrious Klesheim guests as Henry Kissinger.) The art work elsewhere in the palace includes paintings by the baroque court painter Janek, and by the Salzburg-born painters Makart and Eisman.

In all, there are four state apartments; hand-tapestried furniture, a magnificent Venetian secretary of burnt inlay, and an astronomical clock are among their possessions.

Those castle-goers who have not had their fill of Salzburg *Schlösser* with a view of our six can find many others in and around town. A few are open to visitors, like Schloss Arenberg which now houses a museum devoted to Max Reinhardt, while some are in private hands. Probably the most romantic of the latter is Schloss Anif, located south of town, beyond Hellbrunn. With towers, winding staircases, balconies,, pinnacled ballustrades and a bridge leading over a lake of quiet, dark water, it could have come straight out of a Gothic romance. Anif was originally the property of the archbishop Johann Ernst Thun and was remodelled later by a count.

Of historic interest is the complex of buildings in the Old Town known as Chiemseehof which, from the 14th to 19th century, was the residence of the bishops of Chiemsee (now in Bavaria). Being under the jurisdiction of the archbishop of Salzburg – a not always happy relationship – the Chiemsee bishops were required to live six months of the year in Salzburg; hence this dwelling which was re-built in c. 1700. Not long after the secularization of Salzburg, Chiemseehof was a place of refuge for the Spanish prince Don Carlos. Today the provincial *(Land)* government meets here; the *Landeshauptmann,* its top official, has a newly furnished office in what was originally a bedroom of the Chiemsee bishops.

Along the spacious Hellbrunner Allee, lined with centuries-old oak and linden trees, are elegant country houses and small palaces built by the archbishops for their courts, notably Schloss Frohnburg. Also in this lovely neighborhood is Schloss Freisaal, where newly elected archbishops of bygone centuries stayed while awaiting receipt from Rome of the papal pallium, a circular band of wool with pendants; from Freisaal a procession would lead into town.

Considered together, Salzburg's *Schlösser* are very diverse in appearance and intent. Built for defense or fun or show or as a token of love, some are coldly awe-inspiring, others downright inviting. But they do have one clear trait in common: they reveal more vividly than anything else the enormous power and wealth of Salzburg's prince archbishops.

CHAPTER FIVE
A RELIGIOUS HERITAGE

Churches in Salzburg are far more than places of worship. They reflect the dominant role of Catholicism in the days of the prince archbishops. They constitute the predominant architectural factor in the town's overall appearance; indeed, they are its skyline. And in the evolving styles of the churches one can see clearly the passage of the centuries, the changing philosophy of man.

There are remnants still of the romanesque style in Salzburg, with its simple and sombre forms. Rough and plain, the ornamentation does little to detract from the church's only purpose which was to glorify God. By the 12th century this religious fervor had given way to a greater interest in man's own nature and his relation to the universe. Intellectually aware yet fearful of the hereafter, man was, in the gothic period, creating taller, lighter buildings, soaring skyward to reach his master. Today one can find many gothic features of great beauty in Salzburg, even in churches which later were renovated according to newer styles.

The Renaissance, whose spiritual home was the Italian peninsula, blew a refreshing gust of air into late 16th century Salzburg under the rule of Wolf Dietrich. Worldly, emphasizing the glory of man and catering to his pleasures, the Renaissance brought a keen desire for grace and proportion. Now it was not only the church building that counted but the square that it rested upon and the town that held the square. The baroque was but a child of the Renaissance: festive, lavish, sure, man asserting his earthly self even in monuments to God. In the passion for things baroque that overtook Salzburg in the 18th century many churches of earlier periods were modernized – sometimes for the good, at other times not. With the rococo ("baroque with a bit of laughter," the author Czernin calls it, "fluffy little angels floating about on their own special clouds, Madonnas that might start giggling at any moment ..."), the major era of church building was at an end.

Since each church in the town was built for a different congregation, each has its own distinct aura. The Cathedral belonged to the archbishop and was intended to dominate the ecclesiastical scene in height and grandeur. St. Peter's was the monks' sanctuary, the Franciscan a parish church for the townspeople and the Collegiate a part of the university. Early on music became an integral part of the Salzburg church service, and that tradition continues to this day.

Highly professional choirs and orchestras perform the world's finest religious music not only in concert and on high festival days but as part of the regular Sunday mass. Even the church bells are special here. There is no more typically Salzburg sound than that of the pealing bells. Bold, solemn, clarion, insistent, they fill the air with an intense and wonderful cacophony, calling on man to face that which is bigger than himself.

When St. Peter laid the foundation stone of his monastery in the area that became Salzburg, he could hardly have foreseen that this would soon become a renowned center of Christianity and culture and that it would exist, uninterrupted, to this day. Up to the year 987 the archbishopric and St. Peter's remained united, with the monastery taking responsibility for both spiritual and secular affairs. In that year the abbey withdrew from worldly matters to concentrate on art and scholarship – a mission enhanced with the founding in the 17th century of the Benedictine university.

St. Peter's courtyard stands today surrounded by the immense natural framework of the Mönchsberg and dominated by the facade of the church, whose romanesque square tower is crowned by an onion-shaped baroque cupola. Black-garbed Benedictine monks pad quietly back and forth as they have for centuries, past chestnut trees and an ancient covered well and under the archway with the crossed keys, symbol of their own St. Peter who guards the gates of heaven.

The original church burned down and was rebuilt in 12th century romanesque style, but during the baroque heyday it was largely redone. Various abbots have also added their own personal touches to the complex. The result is a comfortable mélange of tastes, with church, chapels, catacombs, graveyard, college, even the wine cellar forming a historically rich and aesthetically delightful area of town.

The entrance to the church is romanesque with alternating blocks of red and white marble; into this is set a lovely rococo door. This is a prime example of the effective merging of architectural styles. The interior continues the rococo splendor, with frescoed ceilings containing delicate pastel stucco work. Wolf Dietrich gave to St. Peter's the handsome Renaissance candlesticks that stand on the altar rail and also the painting of Christ Bearing the Cross by Mennberger on the right wall of the nave. St. Rupert's tomb, the focal point of the church, is on the south aisle, as is the impressive tomb of Wolf

Dietrich's military father. Most of the paintings on the 16 marble altars as well as the high altar are by the master baroque painter known as Kremser-Schmidt.

St. Peter's cemetery, the oldest Christian graveyard in Salzburg, is often cited as the world's most beautiful burial ground. In its present form it dates back to 1627. Enclosed on three sides by wrought iron grilles under baroque arcades which contain chapels belonging to old patrician families of Salzburg, the graveyard is no mournful place. Rather, it is inviting and ageless; here life and death are one and eternity hovers in the ancient rocky walls. The individual graves, many with fine marble tombstones, are lovingly tended, decorated with candles, pine cones, and flowers symmetrically laid upon plots of green. Fir trees, ivy-covered walls and weeping willows overlook the scene, which generally is one of hushed quiet save for the twittering of birds. One can wander here for hours, weaving in and out among the paths. It is especially lovely on certain holy evenings when candles by the graves are lit and in winter "when the snow lies deep in the churchyard and the stark black iron grave markers stand out like charcoal pencils against the drifts" (McGuigan).

Santino Solari, the Cathedral architect is buried here, as are Richard Mayr, beloved local singer who specialized in the operas of Richard Strauss, famous 16th century organist and composer Paul Hofhaymer, builder of the Neutor, Wolfgang Hagenauer, and benefactor Sigmund Haffner. There is a funny story connected with the seven old iron crosses which stand together in St. Peter's cemetery: they are said to be the graves of seven wives dispatched to the other world by the "Bluebeard" of Salzburg who tickled them to death. Actually they are probably the tombs of the Stumpfegger family of stonemasons of whom, in fact, one did die at age 79 after burying six wives.

In the middle of the cemetery is St. Margaret's Chapel, gothic in style; on the floors and walls of this beautiful structure are inlaid tombstones, mostly of Adnet marble. And by the municipal vault in which rest composer Mozart's sister Nannerl and the musician Michael Haydn is the entrance to those fabled Catacombs where the early Christians may have worshipped. Whether or not they did, the feeling within these walls of conglomerate stone is an awesome one. Ascending the steps one reaches first St. Gertrude's Chapel, supposedly from the 4th century and containing niches in the rock where priests could sit; consecrated in 1178 it has been in use ever

73

since. Next is the Maximus Chapel, where the martyr is said to have hidden with his followers, then tiny St. Aegidius Chapel where Rupert is thought to have had his prayer cell. To the right of the Catacombs is the Chapel of the Holy Cross, dating from 1170. A romanesque structure which later became a mausoleum, it stands on the site of the very first abbey church.

Women may not visit the monastery precincts but men may obtain special permission to see the romanesque cloisters, the old gothic chapel of St. Vitus, and the Treasury with its rare church vessels and the oldest library on German soil. Built in 1926 was the College of the Benedictines, whose frescoed facade is by an artist linked particularly with the festival buildings: Anton Faistauer. A huge, starkly realistic crucifix in the vestibule is by the well known Hallein sculptor Jakob Adlhardt.

In the foothills of the Burgberg there exists the female counterpart to St. Peter's: Nonnberg Priory, established by Erentrudis. Life in this oldest nunnery in the world is much as it has always been, its members leading a strict monastic life in the service of God.

In the archway a late gothic statue of Erentrudis welcomes the visitor. The present church, also gothic in style, took the place of an earlier romanesque structure destroyed by fire. Remnants of that first basilica still exist, the most remarkable being several frescoes of saints – dignified, solemn, austere – which are in the nun's choir. The choir is separated from the public parts of the church by an elaborate screen with delicate ornamentation, another example of the fine work done by Salzburg's iron workers. Also noteworthy are the gothic high altar, the stained glass windows and the crypt containing Erentrudis' tomb.

The private quarters for the sisters are plain and dark. They contain many old treasures including handiwork by these women of the Benedictine order and intricate woodcarving. Some of these areas can be seen by special permission. The Chapel of St. John located beside the priory gate contains an exquisite altar piece depicting scenes in the life of the Virgin; it was the gift of Wolf Dietrich. Because Nonnberg is tucked away, high upon a hill in a quiet corner of Salzburg, one feels here an even greater isolation from the world than in St. Peter's. So satisfying is its aura of spiritual peace that a return to town and to our own century can be at first an unwelcome shock.

Salzburg's first Dom (Cathedral), built by Virgil, was consecrated on September 24, 774. (Excavations carried out in our own century revealed the foundations of an even earlier Carolingian building of enormous size on this spot.) Virgil's Cathedral was demolished by fire as were several later wooden constructions – victims of accident or war. A 12th century rebuilding by the archbishop Konrad III resulted in one of the mightiest cathedrals in western Europe.

With Wolf Dietrich and the infamous conflagration that he so welcomed (actually the building was stronger than the fire, so the archbishop had to undermine it with explosives) came the end of Salzburg's medieval Cathedral. The archbishop's grandiose plan, according to designs by Vincenzo Scamozzi or his adopted son, was of the Venetian late Renaissance style and, not surprisingly, would have surpassed in size all the structures that had preceded it. With Wolf Dietrich's downfall, his successor Markus Sittikus had revised plans drawn up for a considerably smaller Cathedral by another North Italian, Santino Solari. Consecrated in Paris Lodron's day, the Cathedral was considered substantially complete by the rule of Max Gandolf, though several baroque features were later added, some of which were removed in an 1859 restoration.

During World War II a bomb crashed through the building's dome and did internal damage as well. After ten years of work the Cathedral was reopened with a weeklong celebration in 1959. Though several interesting new works of art had been executed for the Cathedral during that time, the restoration of the dome itself was not entirely successful.

Salzburg's leading place of worship may not look as Wolf Dietrich envisaged it, but it surely reveals his sweeping grasp of town planning. Carefully situated in direct reference to the Residenz and St. Peter's, it connects with both by three archways of Giovanni Antonio Dario. Intended to be seen from all sides, the three-storey, twin-towered building soars majestic and free in the jewel-like setting of the Domplatz, its rose-tinted Untersberg marble contrasting dramatically with the main construction of dark grey conglomerate stone.

Indeed, there is hardly a more dramatic setting in all of Europe – a fact made clear every summer when the medieval morality play *Everyman* ("Jedermann") is performed in front of the Cathedral during the festival season. This idea of founders Reinhardt and Hugo von Hofmannsthal was a brilliant but also an entirely natural one, for the precedent had been set hundreds of years before when Paris Lodron commissioned the Missa Salisburgensis for the Cathedral consecration. Princes, archdukes, bishops, they were in attendance from all over Europe with their vast retinues, entertained by colored illuminations and fireworks. So important was the event that Paris Lodron decreed a general amnesty of prisoners in the diocese (except for murderers and heretics). In a fashion not unlike our own, he had a huge, lighted image of St. Peter placed upon the fortress. In the center of the river Salzach a fake castle with tower was attacked by two ships until both castle and ships went up in flames. During all of this, feasting and revelry ensued in the town squares for all the populace.

It may sound rather hokey but, in fact, the Cathedral was intended precisely as a setting for such spectacles. Constructed to hold 10,500, the building is an enormous soundingbox whose 10,000-pipe baroque organ sounds best when crowds fill the pews, transforming its cool monumentality into a more human endeavor. Today a high mass shows off the Cathedral best, with priests in their glittering vestments, music filling the air, and the semi-darkness of the nave providing a dramatic contrast to the light streaming in from the dome.

There is much to study in the art and architecture of the building and the square which holds it. In front of the Cathedral portico are oversize statues on high pedestals of apostles Peter and Paul, and at both ends, the local bishop-saints Rupert and Virgil (Rupert has a salt box on his pedestal and Virgil a cathedral on his). On the middle tier above stand the Four Evangelists, on the level above that the two prophets Moses and Elijah, and on the highest central gable, Christ. In the middle of the square is a beautiful Immaculate Column by Salzburg sculptors Johann and Wolfgang Hagenauer.

The interior of the Cathedral, although it was influenced by St. Peter's in Rome, is more closely modeled on the Il Jesu in that city. It is the first church north of the Alps which is of the so-called Italian mannerist style, characterized by a long aisle with choir, galleries and chapels, a transept and central cupola. The arrangement is strong, clearly defined, spacious and geometrically precise. The painting on the apex of the high altar is of the Resurrection, the work of the Florentine Arsenio Mascagni. It, too, is of the mannerist style, with its "cool deliberation in the grouping, emphatic gestures of the figures and typical elongation and attenuation of the naked body" (Paumgartner). On both sides of the high altar are located marble tombs of the archbishops, from Markus Sittikus to Sigismund von Schrattenbach, with memorials to Sittikus and Paris Lodron as the Cathedral's main founders. The former is honored with this macabre text: "Here I, Markus Sittikus... have buried my bones and skin... Scarcely have I reached the roof and I am compelled to go down to the foundation. Death commands..."

The church's bronze doors are quite new, the result of the postwar renovation. They depict the cardinal virtues, faith, hope and charity. Significantly, one of the doors is by an Italian, one by a German, and the last by an Austrian – the three nations most intimately associated with Salzburg's history. While repairing the war damage, architects assigned to the Cathedral decided to rebuild the crypt below. The new construction was carried out in a very innovative way whereby one can see schematically on both floors and walls the plans of both Virgil's and the romanesque cathedrals in relation to the present one.

One concrete remnant from that romanesque time is located at the Cathedral entrance to the left. This is a huge baptismal font, whose pedestal consists of 12th century lions. The bowl itself is gothic (early 14th century) with highly stylized reliefs of bishops and abbots connected with Salzburg. A modern cover was made for the font by Toni Schneider-Manzell, who also designed the new bronze pulpit. Once again, in this single item we find the work of eight centuries blending superbly.

A visit to the Cathedral Treasure Chamber is an important sidelight, for it is a virtual art museum, containing St. Rupert's crosier and travelling flask, a 12th century Limoges Eucharistic dove, costly 12th century mitres, a fine monstrance collection, archbishops' vestments from the 17th and 18th century and baroque chalices. Special exhibits are also housed here.

When Wolf Dietrich had Salzburg's cemetery dug up in order to make room for his great new city squares, it was St. Sebastian's in the New Town that was to become the main resting place for the deceased. The archbishop did not carry out the changeover with particular grace, directing that various bodies which had been reposing peacefully in the Cathedral grounds be dumped on their former doorsteps or simply flung into the Salzach.

The new graveyard was conceived with the same creativity that characterized all his architectural schemes. Enlarging the cemetery that was already there, Wolf Dietrich redesigned it in the style of an

Italian *campo santo* (literally, "open field") – less a place of solemnity for the dead than one of pleasant contemplation for the living. (In this it is not dissimilar to the cemetery at St. Peter's.) Hidden and secluded, it remains today just footsteps away from the city congestion.

Buried in the mausoleum of Gabriel's Chapel in the middle of the cemetery is Wolf Dietrich himself. His coffin can be seen through a small iron grill in the floor – a startlingly vivid reminder of the long-deceased dreamer. The round structure, surmounted by a cupola and designed by Elia Castello, is ironically, the only building that this archbishop saw to completion. The interior walls are full of richly colored, checkered tile and stucco work; four lavishly decorated niches hold oversize statues of the Evangelists. Renaissance in style and Spanish in feeling, the chapel is a bizarre sight, standing proudly in the grey-toned, moss-grown graveyard.

Wolf Dietrich was very specific about how he was to be buried: simply. These instructions were not to be carried out, however; his successor Markus Sittikus (who had helped to depose him) dictated a ceremony with full regal splendor. In any case, we find inscribed here at St. Gabriel's Wolf Dietrich's precise burial instructions: "He shall be dressed in his everyday clothes; the servants who attended him during his darkest days are to put his body into the earth; they are to walk at the head of the funeral procession bearing only one cross and four candles; only six monks of the holy Franciscan order and nobody else are to accompany him; all this is to be done at night ..."

Another man buried at St. Sebastian's is the Swiss physician/alchemist/occultist/astrologist Paracelsus. Born near Zurich in 1493 and christened Theophrastus Bombastus von Hohenheim, he took the name Paracelsus after a Roman physician and spent most of his life as a wandering scholar and healer, writing erudite tomes and seeking the elixir of life. Eventually he was invited by another student of the occult, the archbishop Ernst Duke of Bavaria* to settle in Salzburg, which he did, first at Platzl 3 and then at an inn at Kaigasse 8 where he died in 1541.

---

* A much later archbishop, the 18th century Count of Dietrichstein, was also enamoured of things chemical. During an experiment he unknowingly created a quicksilver-like poison which caused his skin to open in great wounds. The advice given him for the malady was to cover his entire body and face with gold leaf. This done, he proceeded to die of asphixiation.

Paracelsus was a cocky, vulgar, noisy, belligerent man (the word "bombast" derives from his middle name). Fat and bald, he dressed like a tramp and had a face red from heavy drinking. Disdainful of his colleagues, he insulted them with choice obscenities, and hence found himself thrown out of more than one town. No wonder it was rumored that, in Salzburg, he died by being pushed off a cliff or poisoned, though in fact he was probably just tired out. (According to the poison story, a great bird was seen entering his lodgings where, with its beak, it removed the venomous knot that had collected in his throat).

Despite his well earned unpopularity, there was more to Paracelsus than bombast, for he had an uncanny scientific instinct and was not far removed from our present-day approach to medicine. The magical ability for healing that he unquestionably had was based upon the recognition that man is a microcosm of nature and man's health dependent on a harmony with nature. He, as physician, was only a vessel of God, for, he believed, the greatest healer of all was nature itself. A passionate, magnetic, empirical, tough-minded man, Paracelsus was famous for curing ailments as diverse as dropsy and paralysis, leprosy and gangrene. He evidently relieved the great scholar Erasmus of kidney disease and gout. Paracelsus strove after a religious ideal of poverty. In his will he left all his possessions to the poor and infirm of Salzburg. He is honored today not only by his splendid tombstone but by the Kurhaus in the Mirabell Gardens which is named after him (mud and mineral waters, hydrotherapy, etc.). An annual meeting of researchers in the International Paracelsus Society meets here and, in true Salzburg fashion, a drugstore, a boutique and wine cellar are all named after the vagrant healer.

Among the other graves of interest at St. Sebastian's are those of the architect of Gabriel's Chapel, the wife and father of Wolfgang Amadeus Mozart, and the mother of Salome Alt.

The church itself dates from the 18th century; it was built upon the site of a much older building. The newer version was severely damaged in the 1818 fire that devastated so much of Salzburg.

Of all Salzburg's places of worship, the Franziskanerkirche ("Church of the Franciscans"), whose graceful, tall spire is immediately recognizable from all over town, encompasses perhaps the greatest diversity of architectural styles. Such may well have resulted in a lack of harmony but, in fact, the church is exquisite and, for many people, surpasses all others in its nobility. The ever poetic Bahr wrote "Whoever leaves by the Southern door has experienced the whole history of Christian architecture and the stones call to him the words of Goethe: 'We belong to those who strive from darkness into light.'"

There was a church on this spot dedicated to Our Lady even in the time of St. Virgil. It burned down and a new one was consecrated with a romanesque nave, which still exists, as do other romanesque features such as a stone lion set into the steps of the pulpit. Then, in the early 15th century, the town's rich burghers to whom the church belonged felt it had become old-fashioned, and so they had the choir rebuilt in gothic style by the Master of Burghausen – and a master he was – also known as Hans Stethaimer. In this fusion lies one of the church's wonders: the heavy, sombre romanesque of the basilica which gives way to the light-flooded, delicate choir, completed later with reticulated vaulting supported by five slender pillars.

In 1495 the great Tyrolean wood artist Michael Pacher was summoned to create a new winged high altar. He worked on the shimmering golden panels and slim figures of saints until his death. From all accounts, this was one of his masterpieces, equal to his altar at the church in the Salzkammergut town of St. Wolfgang. But all we have today to judge it by is the sweetfaced Madonna, one of Salzburg's single greatest treasures. For the baroque style had swept in and gothic was ordered out. Fortunately, the man hired to effect the transformation was not only a superb artist in his own right but one who respected the past: Fischer von Erlach. Retaining the Pacher limewood Madonna, he created for her a splendid baroque heaven in which she sits enthroned, flanked by St. George and St. Florian. In its great height, his own altar integrates harmoniously with the gothic chancel. As for the rest of Pacher's work, the gold and silver were melted down and sold at a pittance.

Other indignities befell the lovely church. Max Gandolf, for instance, lopped off the pointed cupola of the tower, replacing it with a lower baroque cover. His reason? The cupola of this, the disdained people's church, competed with the towers of the Cathedral, which was *his* church. (Much later, a neo-gothic tower was constructed.) And then that shabby ruler of Mozart's time, Hieronymus von Colloredo, decided to play Wolf Dietrich and expand the Residenz; such would entail turning the nave of the Franciscan Church into a stable and the choir into his own personal mausoleum. Fortunately, Napoleon came along and put an end to some of his schemes.

Kleßheim Palace — international meeting place for presidents (Nixon, Ford and Sadat have been here) and kings . . .

The Provincial Governor of Salzburg has his offices in the former palace of the Chiemsee Bishops (below), Kupferstichkabinett.

The Fortress Hohensalzburg has become a symbol of the city (above). The view from the east shows the Nonnberg Convent (featured in the »Sound of Music«) and the transport of salt along the river Salzach.

The regal rooms in the Fortress Hohensalzburg have survived many centuries, and also the so-called »Golden Stove«, a masterpiece of Salzburg ceramic art.

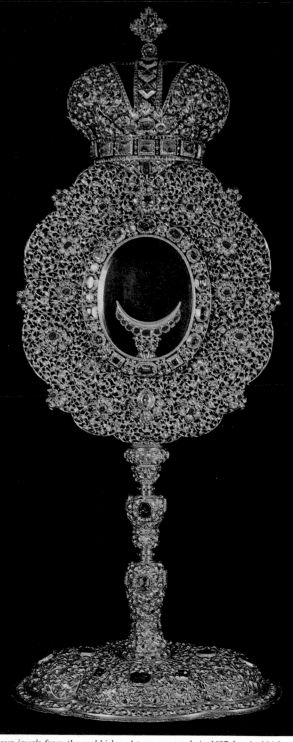

The monstrance of precious jewels from the archbishops' treasury, made in 1697 for Archbishop Johann Ernst Graf Thun (Cathedral Museum). Made of gold, 75 cm high, inlaid with 1,792 diamonds, 24 emeralds, 405 rubies and other precious stones.

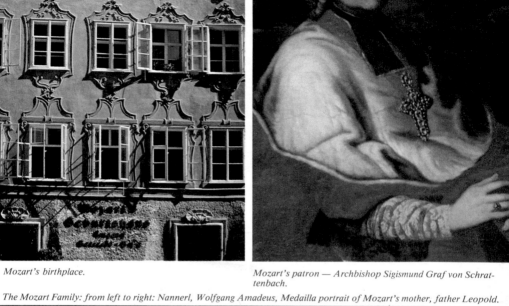

Mozart's birthplace.

Mozart's patron — Archbishop Sigismund Graf von Schrattenbach.

The Mozart Family: from left to right: Nannerl, Wolfgang Amadeus, Medailla portrait of Mozart's mother, father Leopold.

The most important musician and composer at the court of Emperor Maximilian was the Salzburger Paul Hofhaimer, shown here on the organ waggon of a triumphant imperial march (1517).

University Hall built in 1631. About 600 performances of the Benedictine Theatre were given here from 1622 — 1776 (below).

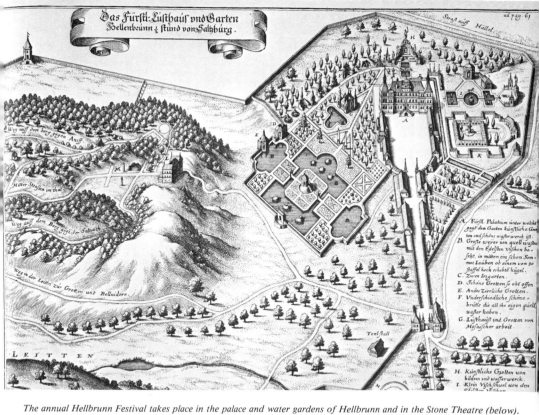

Das Fürstl. Lusthauß vnd Garten
Hellenbrunn ¼ stund von Salzburg.

ad pag. 63

Straß auff Hallel

Weg auff den berg gegen Auß

Mitter Straßen im thal

Weg auff den Berg gegen Selhach

Weg in der Leitten zur Grotten und Belluidere.

LEITTEN

Tenlstall

A. Fürstl. Palatium unter welchet gegst dem Garten kunstliche Gnetten vnd schöne wasserwerck ist.
B. Grosse weyer von quell wasser mit den Edelsten Vischen besetzt, in mitten ein schön Sommer Lauben ob einen von 30 staffel hoch erhebt hügel.
C. Zwen Irgarten.
D. Schöne Grotten so ob offen.
E. Andre Zierliche Grotten.
F. Vnderschiedliche schöne brünne die all ihr eigen quell wasser haben.
G. Lusthauß und Grotten von Mosaischer arbeit.

H. Kunstliche Grotten von bilden vnd wasserwerck.
I. Klein Vischhäusel von Glä...

The annual Hellbrunn Festival takes place in the palace and water gardens of Hellbrunn and in the Stone Theatre (below).

The mystery play »Jedermann« by Hugo von Hofmannsthal, performed on the Cathedral Square is one of the annual highlights of the Salzburg Festival.

J. B. Fischer von Erlach – the name runs through the fabric of Salzburg's architectural history, an ever present thread. Who was he and why was he so important? In the eyes of one biographer, at least, Hans Aurenhammer: "It was due to him that Austria, after having been virtually an Italian province in the realm of art and architecture for almost two centuries became suddenly at the end of the 17th century a focal point of artistic achievement once more."

Born in 1656 in Graz to a notable burgher family, he grew up in the tradition of Styrian craftsmanship, training under his sculptor father. As a youth he went to study in Rome, then Naples, returning home 16 years later, a man of the world. In the meantime, Austria had become a great European power.

Salzburg, in those years still an independent archbishopric, afforded him the greatest opportunity for developing his gifts as a builder of churches and a town planner. Toward the end of the 17th century, Italian-style architecture by such men as Gaspare Zugalli had been popular, but archbishop Johann Ernst Graf Thun had an aversion to the Italian style, hiring Fischer to be his architectural advisor and inspector of buildings. He treated his new employee well, providing him with a hefty annual sum in florins and a considerable amount of wine from his own estate. As time went on, the domes and towers of Fischer's churches gradually changed the Salzburg skyline, and other works took form, too, one after another: stables, hospital, as well as castle gardens.

His first commission to build a church was Salzburg's Dreifaltigkeitskirche ("Holy Trinity Church"). Dominated by a lofty, oval-shaped dome, the inside of which was painted by that busy ceiling artist Rottmayr, this church was the result of the archbishop's concern that Salzburg's New Town was developing in a haphazard fashion. With the Dreifaltigkeitskirche he wanted to create order by introducing a grand-style baroque arrangement on the Makartplatz.

Fischer succeeded admirably, placing the church between two plain wings that had other ecclesiastical functions, the result being a fine architectural unity. The interior is small but perfectly proportioned, surmounted by its dome which seems to open the church to the sky above. Unfortunately, that terrible fire to which we have often referred took much of the church with it, and it was reconstructed with different towers.

Severely damaged in a far larger tragedy, World War II, was Fischer's Ursuline Church. The Ursuline nuns were brought to Salzburg by archbishop Johann Thun to set up a school for children.

For them Fischer built a special church with dainty ceiling ornamentation and a lovely curved gallery. This was the most richly
adorned of all his ecclesiastical buildings.

The Kollegienkirche ("University" or "Collegiate Church"),
consecrated in 1707, is Fischer von Erlach's masterpiece of this
genre in Salzburg, as well as one of the finest examples of the Austrian baroque. Full of vitality and originality and very personal in
quality, it may at first seem cold and barren, but increased familia-
rity with it convinces one of its majestic nobility, the soaring, simple
lines. In Schmiedbauer's view, the Kollegienkirche reveals "a sculptor's striving for form as well as the consummate mastery of the
architect."

According to the gossip of the day, the conditions under which
the church was built were less than felicitous. The archbishop had
been involved in a longtime feud with the wealthy and noble Kuenburg family whose palace stood near University Square and, to spite
them, had the church built up right against the walls of their man-
sion, shutting off both light and air. True or not, the result makes
the exact origins seem less significant.

The facade of the church features handsome towers which culmi-
nate in eight statues set against the sky. On the gable over the entrance is a figure of the Immaculate Conception. Inside, open space
is used to great dramatic effect and there is no unnecessary ornamentation. The church is without aisles, in the shape of a Greek
cross with the huge dome above the axis. In the angles of the cross
are four oval-shaped chapels, each dedicated to the patron saint of a
faculty within the university. Altars in the chapels were painted by
Rottmayr.

Among the most inspired features is the apse behind the high altar, on whose wall is depicted a fine stucco creation of a baroque
heaven with saints and angels floating around the figure of the Virgin; stucco work is by Carlo Diego Carlone and Paolo de Allio.
Again Schmiedbauer: "All sense of earthly reality is dispelled in the
darkness of the apse, where the architectural proportions are ob-
scured by representations of clouds, a vision of eternity dissolving
into celestial glory."

An interesting detail about the University Church – it is the only
house of God in the Old Town that does not face west.

As time went on and the eyes of archbishop Johann Ernst Thun
began to fail, he saw only dimly the wonders that his chosen architect had wrought. But he must have remained pleased to the end, for

upon his death his heart was buried in a heart-shaped silver urn in Holy Trinity Church, his brain in University Church and his bowels in the Hospital Church of John the Baptist – all Fischer buildings. With the archbishop's passing, Fischer lost one of his most generous and understanding patrons.

During the last decade of the 17th century a considerable number of buildings were erected according to Fischer's designs but without his actual presence, both in Salzburg and many other cities. His two single most famous buildings are the Karlskirche and Schönbrunn Palace, both in Vienna; the latter design was so monumental that it proved financially impossible for even the Habsburg court to execute. A pity, for it was to have left all other palaces, including Versailles, in the shade.

About his private life we do not know a great deal. Married to the daughter of a notary who gave him five children, Fischer was widowed and remarried to a woman who deserted him. He thereupon disowned the faithless lady, leaving his money toward the founding of almshouses. Of his children, one became a worthy collaborator. Fischer was raised to the nobility in 1696, a friend and confidant to philosophers, emperors, scientists and artists throughout Europe.

Together Fischer's buildings bespeak his artistic credo. "He saw himself as part of a living stream of architectural development and as one who was completing ideas which began in antiquity" (Aurenhammer). An idealist and a man of broad cultural knowledge, he strove for absolute perfection. God to him was the greatest of all architects who had created the world as a perfect building. The emperor (and archbishop) were representatives of God's majesty on earth. A building did not stand alone, but as part of the harmonic structure of the landscape. Figurative arts were subordinate to the architecture. Buildings were planned so that the inner structure could be clearly seen from the outside.

Fischer had no real successors and founded no school. No sculptor or painter who collaborated with him even remotely approached his level though Rottmayr, for one, was much in sympathy with his aims.

He was unique and so are his buildings.

Among the many Catholic orders which made a home in Salzburg on the invitation of an archbishop were the Theatine monks, invited here by Max Gandolf. The order had been founded by St. Cajetan, the most renowned Catholic theologian of his day, who had tried unsuccessfully to talk Martin Luther into returning to the church.

The exquisitely proportioned Cajetan church by architect Gaspare Zugalli has a yellow, *palazzo*-like exterior, a huge central dome and – in accordance with the order's laws – no flanking towers. It is a typical product of the Italian baroque. Inside, the finest painting is Rottmayr's vigorous depiction of the Holy Family on the left side of the altar. At the side of the church is a hospital and Collegium – the most striking example in Salzburg of a common feature whereby houses of worship (with the notable exception of the Cathedral) do not stand alone but connect and blend with neighboring buildings in a tasteful manner that combines art with utility, sacred with secular.

By the same architect is the Church of St. Erhard, also baroque in style. It is entered through a stately portico raised above street level because of floods which at one time occurred frequently in this Nonntal area. The adjacent wings used to serve as a hospital for attendants of the archbishop. Artwork on the high altar is by Rottmayr and the stucco work of Francesco Brenno, largely terracotta in color, is rich and lively.

Crowning the Kapuzinerberg is the modest gold-beige monastery of another order, the Capuchin, dating from the time of Wolf Dietrich. Its doors are thought to have been brought here from the romanesque Cathedral. This was a favorite spot of the archbishop Paris Lodron.

It was he who built the companion Loreto Church in the New Town for a group of Capuchin nuns, refugees from the Thirty Years War. The greatest treasure here is the Salzburger Kindl ("Little Child of Salzburg"),* a tiny ivory figure many hundreds of years old. Considered a miraculous image, the beautiful figure is elegantly clothed in garments studded with precious jewels. Several outfits were created, each denoting a holy occasion; the change of attire is carried out upon a bed with great ceremony. For centuries believers came here to touch the head of the Christ Child figure with their own, for this, they believed, would restore their health. Important citizens could request that the Child be brought to their homes for this purpose and, if the suffering was too great to bear, the Child might be supplicated for a peaceful death. It must have been a remarkable sight – the tiny image being placed in a carriage and sent,

---

* Information on Salzburger Kindl, courtesy Frau Nora Watteck.

accompanied by guards, to a burgher's home. Even today there are peasants who continue to venerate the image, which is the only one of its kind in Austria.

The convent of San Loreto is the strictest in Salzburg and the one most closed to outsiders, even to the families of the nuns. Traditionally, the sisters hoped to die quickly, avoiding purgatory and going straight to heaven. Hence, while eating they would overlook a decomposing, vermin-filled sarcophagus which represented the meaninglessness of food and life itself; similarly, at night they slept in a coffin to hasten the desired event, death.

Today few enter the walls of Loreto Convent – the life is simply too difficult. But nowhere is the monastic life an easy one. Even at Nonnberg the nuns are not allowed to leave their cells after eight p.m.; if they become ill during the night, a physician cannot be summoned till morning.

There are many other churches of historical and architectural interest in and around Salzburg. St. Michael's, the original parish church, was founded in 800; the present rose-colored building dates from the 18th century.

Located in picturesque fashion upon a spur of the Mönchsberg is the parish church of Mülln. Consecrated in 1453, the Gothic structure was later redecorated in elaborate early rococo. Wolf Dietrich was responsible for the flying arch that bridges the church with the old Augustine Monastery – famous for its beer – across the street. Legend has it that the archbishop had himself and Salome Alt depicted as Mary and Joseph in the painting of the Holy Family in the rear chapel.

Clinging to the cliff of the same Mönchsberg is tall, narrow St. Blasius. Gothic in style and dating from the 14th century, for many years it served as a place of worship connected with the Town Hospital.

One of the most pleasant short excursions form Salzburg is to the twin-towered pilgrimage church of Maria Plain, which stands on a hill about two miles to the north of town. The fine baroque place of worship, replacing a wooden chapel, was erected by Max Gandolf to plans of Giovanni Dario. Its purpose was to house a likeness of the Virgin that supposedly had been responsible for many healings – another miraculous image. One of the most richly decorated churches in Austria, Maria Plain is especially popular for weddings, and no wonder. It shimmers with gold, silver and candles, and offers a superb view of the cityscape. Along the road leading to the church are four Calvary chapels.

Given the dominance of the Catholic church, it is hardly surprising that places of worship for other faiths are not many in Salzburg. The small Protestant population now worships at a Lutheran church in the Schwarzstrasse or at Taxham, and the Jewish synagogue, torn down and rebuilt many times, is presently in the Lasserstrasse.

Having seen a good number of Salzburg's churches, the visitor may be struck with an unexpected realization: that here, unlike many other cities, the overall effect of these most serious of buildings is neither one of gloom nor heaviness but of life and joy. Is this once again the indescribable harmony between landscape and architecture, or the cheerful influence from Italy to the south, or is it the dominant presence of the baroque? Hermann Bahr sees it unquestionably as the last. The baroque, for him "is movement, is life itself ... as fleeting as music and as everlasting... Whereas in other places one cannot but suffer a certain anguish, even pity, when face to face with old relics, standing alone and forgotten in a strange world, here one feels the age-old still to be with us."

CHAPTER SIX
MOZART THEN AND NOW

"Music's genius of light and love." That is how Wolfgang Amadeus Mozart was described by a later and far different composer: Richard Wagner. It is an apt phrase – insofar as any words are capable of reflecting the glory of Mozart's music. Scholars refer to him as "supernational": far beyond national boundaries or limitations, as being the most flawless and natural of musicians. They point to the "thread" that unifies the individual movements of his works. For many, his creations – pure, serene and godlike – stand at heaven's gates. Indeed, today, almost two and a half centuries after his birth in Salzburg, Mozart is for a large number of serious listeners the greatest composer who ever lived.

The definitive Köchel catalogue which lists chronologically all of Mozart's known compositions, including those which have been lost, specifies 626 separate works. As miraculous as the sheer ease and speed with which these were dispatched (after all, he lived not even to age 36) is their depth. The inspired quality of Mozart's writing becomes all the more unfathomable when we remember that the bulk of his music was produced on command or commission.

There was no contemporary form of significance that Mozart did not master. His own favorite was opera, a medium that enabled him to reveal fully his powers of psychological insight. In these richly varied works – 23 in all – Mozart tells us a great deal about man's capacity for good and evil, strength and weakness, joy and sorrow.

Mozart wrote a great number of religious compositions; these were part of his job. But they were also a part of his being and reflect his own relationship with the hereafter. Raising "neither a humble prayer nor a Promethean challenge to the gods," (Will Durant) these creations are direct, humane, devout in an unquestioning, childlike faith, even festive; such characteristics apply as well to the church architecture of this time.

Mozart's knowledge of individual instruments was supreme. It may be that the summit of his musical activity lay in the 27 piano concerti which some critics feel to be the apotheosis of the piano. In these, orchestra and solo instrument are treated with a brilliant equality; the melodies of the slow movements are marvels of simplicity, of sublime rightness. And in his sonatas Mozart was the first modern master to balance two frequently non-complementary instruments: piano and violin.

Most composers are superficial in light forms such as minuets, marches, night music, but Mozart offers here some of his most precious thoughts. As a scintillating mirror of secular life in his time, Mozart's "entertainment" music is unmatched.

Finally and this listing by no means exhausts the forms Mozart undertook – are the 41 symphonies. Most are not in today's repertoire, but certain ones, like the "Prague" and "Haffner" are staples of the concert hall, and the last three (E flat major, G minor, and C major) show perhaps most dramatically the extraordinary facility, the fertility of his musical imagination, for they were all produced in the incredibly short space of six weeks. Works of almost violently contrasting key and mood, they marked the last black, desperate summer of his short life.

The basic facts about the life of the man who was christened Johannes Chrysostomus Wolfgangus Theophilus (Amadeus) Mozart are as well known as any in the annals of music. He was born January 27, 1756, in the street Getreidegasse to Leopold Mozart and his wife Anna Maria, née Pertl. The father was a violinist and court composer for archbishop Sigismund von Schrattenbach. His own compositions were popular but ordinary; far more noteworthy was the book he wrote on violin technique. The mother was a gentle woman, devoted to home and family.

Wolfgang showed very early his remarkable gifts, playing the piano and violin and composing when most children were chanting nursery rhymes. When he was six, Wolfgang was considered ready for presentation to the musical world along with his talented older sister Nannerl.* Their first trip was to Munich, the next to Vienna where the children charmed Empress Maria Theresia with a keyboard performance at Schönbrunn Castle. Before long, father, son and daughter were on the road more than they were at home. Italy, Holland, France, England, Switzerland, Belgium – individual trips lasted as long as three years and brought ecstatic responses from audiences in every city. It was a heady life for the boy: having his harpsichord and violin sonatas published in Paris at age 8, commissioned by the Emperor Joseph II to write an opera at 12, knighted in Italy at 14 and in the same year made leader of the archbishop's orchestra at home, with frequent assignments to write liturgical works for the Catholic service.

---

* Five other Mozart children had died at birth or infancy.

Throughout all this and later Leopold was his only teacher. As the greatest single influence on Wolfgang's life, he has been the subject of much discussion, pro and con. There is no question that Leopold saw clearly his son's genius and devoted his own life to developing it, first as teacher, then as self-proclaimed servant. Whether this amounted to exploitation is another matter. In any case, Wolfgang was a willing pupil – at least until many years later when his father's domineering manner began to rankle. And the travel was a matchless form of music education for the boy, though it brought such travails as a bout with scarlet fever which almost killed him (as well as Nannerl) and which may well have contributed to his early death of probable kidney disease.

The first archbishop with whom the Mozarts were associated, Sigismund von Schrattenbach, was an easy-going (except to heretics), patriarchal master, with an interest in music. A bit suspicious at first that Mozart Senior was cooperating in his son's composing, he invited the boy at age eleven to live with him in isolation for a week and to compose part of an oratorio in that time. It was done and Sigismund became convinced of the boy's ability. To his credit, the archbishop not only did not object to the long tours of father and son but donated some funds toward the Italian trip, bestowing upon Wolfgang an appropriate title for his travels: concertmaster of the court music.*

Given the excitement of life on the road, it is not surprising that the young Mozart found daily existence in Salzburg to be a drag. But as he approached adolescence, even foreign audiences reacted rather less worshipfully than they had before. And a new element had entered the picture: jealousy. By the time Wolfgang was twelve, musicians in Vienna were looking upon him not as *Wunderkind* (child prodigy) but rival.

* This benevolent attitude, while not common, had its precedents. Two and a half centuries before, a certain Paul Hofhaymer, organist and composer who was Salzburg's first musician of European reputation, developed such a close relationship with the Kaiser Maximilian that he was known as the "Kaiser's truest companion." The two traveled frequently on music-making journeys, and it was said of them that "they had their home in the saddle." (Bresgen, writting in the book *"In Salzburg geboren".*)

In 1771 Sigismund died and the 40 year old enlightened despot Hieronymus von Colloredo donned the archbishop's robes. From then on, life in the archiepiscopal court was intolerable for the Mozarts. No friend of the arts, stingy Hieronymus wanted to cut down on the church trimmings – and these included music. Masses, even the most solemn, were not to exceed 45 minutes, father and son were told, but must be scored for all instruments. Nor did Hieronymus take kindly to the idea of his two servants running off for tours, which he referred to as "begging expeditions." At first he merely withheld Leopold's salary. Then, in 1777, he refused to grant the father's leave, saying that as a half-time servant Wolfgang (then concertmaster, on the pay of a clerk) could go alone. When the Mozarts seemed ready to take him up on this, Hieronymus raised new objections. Wolfgang asked for his own dismissal, reminding the archbishop that "the Gospel teaches one to use his talents for the improvement of our own and our parents' circumstances." A sarcastic employer decided to rid himself of both troublemakers: "... father and son in accordance with the Gospel, have permission to seek their fortune elsewhere." Leopold begged for indulgence, and his own dismissal was cancelled.

Wolfgang set off for Paris with his mother, who died in that city – the first heartbreak of the composer's life. And the trip brought none of the hoped-for concrete rewards.

When he returned home, the family had no options left; they petitioned Hieronymus von Colloredo to appoint Wolfgang to a different position: court organist. Leopold drew up the petition: "Your Serene Highness, Most Reverend Prince of the Empire ..." Wolfgang signed it, and the archbishop granted the request.

Mozart remained in court service until 1781, becoming ever more frustrated with the limitations it imposed on his great talents. Fortunately there were distractions, such as a commission from Munich for an opera, the result being *Idomeneo*. But these could not compensate for the misery of working at Hieronymus' court. And Leopold's continued intrusion in his son's life on matters romantic and musical were no longer appreciated.

The final break between master and servant occurred when Wolfgang, having accompanied the archbishop to Vienna for a series of concerts (he was placed at the table with only the cooks beneath him) refused to return to Salzburg on the designated date, because he wanted to seek out new possibilities in Vienna. The archbishop insisted that he had a special letter to entrust to him. Mozart refused and Hieronymus von Colleredo exploded. Mozart wrote to his father, "He gave me bad names to my face, he called me a scamp, a scoundrel, a playboy, a blighter, a fool ..." The insulted musician tried to resign but his archbishop would not give him the desired walking papers. "You allow yourself to be far too easily dazzled by Vienna," remarked Count Arco, Mozart's immediate superior in the court service. The composer persisted; after his third request Arco simply – and literally – kicked him out. Interestingly, no formal dismissal came then or later, but Mozart was not about to wait for it. He remained in Vienna for the rest of his short life, while Leopold continued in the archiepiscopal service. As for Hieronymus von Colloredo, he lived until the age of 80, witnessing the growing posthumous fame of his insolent organist.

History has understandably been hard on the archbishop. Yet one musicologist, the eminent scholar Alfred Einstein, paints a more human portrait. He reminds us that with all their absences the Mozarts were of little use to the court. Einstein calculates that between January 1762 and March 1773 father and son were out of town for a total of seven years. Had their master recognized that one of the two was a genius, perhaps he would have acted differently – or perhaps not. What he wanted was a conscientious, faithful worker, not a peripatetic prodigy. This attitude can be regretted, says Einstein, as can the man's stupidity (he advised Mozart that study in Naples might do much to rectify his serious musical shortcomings) but not condemned. And, claims Einstein, the archbishop seems not to have made Leopold suffer for his son's wilfulness.

Research presently being conducted in Vienna may add another dimension to the story. It concerns possible connivance between Leopold and the archbishop, aimed at keeping Wolfgang in Salzburg where the father could retain a hold over both his music and his marital prospects. If, indeed this was their plan, it did not succeed.

Hugo von Hofmannsthal, co-founder of Salzburg's summer music festival, made this comment: "It was inevitable that Mozart should have been born here [in Salzburg] in the heart of Europe. It lies halfway between Switzerland and the Slav countries, halfway between northern Germany and transalpine Italy, between mountains and plains, between the heroic and the idyllic. Its architecture is a marriage of town and country, old and new, noble and homely. Mozart is the exact expression of all this. In Central Europe there is no place more beautiful."

That remark may well be true, but it doubtless would not have found a supporter in Mozart himself, as the composer had few kind words for his native city from his earliest years to his last. One might expect that its physical beauty, at least, would have evoked his enthusiasm, but there were other lovely towns nearby which made Salzburg seem not so unique, and anyway, he was not a composer for whom surroundings mattered a great deal. He received his inspiration from within rather than from the streams and hills and storms that nourished a Schubert, Handel, Beethoven. As a matter of fact, Mozart was never particularly attracted to any locale, preferring to be on the go (in a closed coach) where he could look ahead to new scenery – the musical kind. No, his reaction to Salzburg had simply to do with what it could offer him as a musician, and that, unfortunately, was not much. Frequent travels to towns like Mannheim, whose creative life was much more advanced, did not help matters, nor did the increasingly tense relationship with the archiepiscopal court. Mozart began to make fun of Salzburg early on, and from the age of about 16 he quite simply loathed it.

Granted, Salzburg was full of music – for the church, drawing room, theater – but the quality of composition, performance and audience was on the whole mediocre. The preference was for coarse, naturalistic music, heavy on humor – rather like that composed by Leopold. (Wolfgang's compositions, ever freer of tradition and steeped in his own personality, would never satisfy such demands).

Mozart made no secret of the mutual dislike. "I refuse to associate with a good many people there – and most of the others do not think me good enough. Besides, there is no stimulus for my talent: When I play or when any of my compositions are performed, it is just as if the audience were all tables and chairs." Nor were the performers capable of adequately interpreting his works. "In the first place," wrote Mozart to the Abbé Bullinger, "professional musicians there are not held in much consideration; secondly, one hears nothing, there is no theater, no opera; and even if they really wanted one, who is there to sing? For the last five or six years, the Salzburg orchestra has always been rich in what is useless and absolutely destitute in what is indispensable." (The useless in this case was another soprano and the indispensable, a conductor.) Salzburg was simply "no place for my talent."

92

Yet Wolfgang could never exorcize Salzburg from his being. Many positive aspects of his personality and his music – the gay, witty side, the aristocratic tone, the inherent sense of harmony – derive in part from the town he renounced. And, in retrospect, the Salzburg period of Mozart's creative life was one of stunning achievement – especially in view of his youth: serenades, divertimenti (the one named for Countess Lodron, for instance), symphonies, masses, motets, oratorios, piano sonatas, four-handed piano selections, operas and his crowning work in the field of the violin concerto, K.364 in E-flat major.

By the time he moved to Vienna, Mozart was disenchanted not only with Salzburg but with the world of music as a whole. He had tried many times without success to find a good position.

The few chances that came his way (one of them as organist at Versailles) he had turned down for reasons which, in Leopold's practical mind, at least, had no validity, and for other positions he was bypassed, perhaps because his work was too individual to be understood. Now he was on his own, and with no employment.

In Vienna, life suddenly began to look up. Here Mozart had his first great adult success, as composer of the gay play with music, *Il Seraglio*. With this one work, set in Turkey, he became the most sought after musician in town. Shortly after the première, without Leopold's consent, he married Constanze Weber, the sister of an earlier flame, whose family had taken advantage of the ardent musician's generosity – and gullibility. He apparently remained devoted to Constanze, who was neither a good housewife nor companion in his life's work. Of their six children, only two boys lived to maturity.

Vienna also brought Mozart some welcome success as a performer (he may well have been the greatest keybord virtuoso of his day) and conductor of his own works. He was at his most creative, works fairly flying from his pen: among them, the C Minor Mass, six string quartets, *The Marriage of Figaro*. The latter opera closed quickly, however, in Vienna for, despite favorable reviews, the social criticism inherent in the play from which it was taken did not please the mighty.

In 1787 Mozart's father became seriously ill. The son's affection poured forth in a letter: "I hope and trust that while I am writing this, you are feeling better. But if... you are not recovering, I implore you not to hide it from me, so that as quickly as is humanly possible, I may come to your arms." It was too late. Leopold died before they could meet again. He would have loved Wolfgang's next big work, another opera: *Don Giovanni*. This great *dramma giocoso* (from the Italian, literally "merry drama") took Prague, where it was premièred, by storm; not so Vienna.

In fact, Vienna, like Salzburg, by now had let him down. For one thing, his new compositions for chamber groups were too difficult to be played by amateurs, who lost interest. The last three great symphonies of which we have spoken were most likely not performed at all during his lifetime. And even when a work was both performed and well received – his final opera, that glorious fairy tale in music, *The Magic Flute*, was the rage of Vienna – his name as composer was sometimes omitted entirely from the program, at other times appeared in the smallest type. The title Mozart had been able to win in Vienna, of Royal and Imperial Court Composer, sounded important, but it brought only an honorary stipend. Pupils dwindled. Then he was excluded from the official retinue at the crowning of Leopold II in Frankfurt. With the deterioration of his financial position, he was forced to beg sums of money from a fellow member of the freemason's society in order to stave off the creditors.

That was not all. Mozart was ill – with chills, fever, swelling, the symptoms of what was probably uraemia. By September of 1791 he sensed the end was near. "The hour has struck. I must die. I am at an end now, before I could enjoy my talent." His sensibilities, always acute, were now painfully sharp. Even the song of his pet canary was too much for him to bear; it had to be removed from earshot.

In July 1791 the bailiff of a certain count appeared at Mozart's lodgings, requesting that he write a Requiem in memory of said count's dead wife; Mozart would be paid but the count would claim it as his own. Mozart accepted the commission, telling friends that it was his own Requiem he was writing. On the last day of his life he asked for the score and, with three visitors, sang the completed parts, weeping when he came to the "Lacrimosa." He died December 5.

The next day his body was taken to St. Stephan's Cathedral where it was blessed, and then he was buried in a mass grave at St. Marx. Only a handful of friends attended. When Constanze came a few days later to pray, no one could tell her where her husband's remains lay.

Prague mourned the man Vienna had so quickly forgotten. Some 4,000 of its citizens turned out to honor the memory of the "German Apollo" with a performance of his Requiem (it had been completed by a composer named Süssmayr).

Mozart's death mask and all reproductions of it have crumbled to bits.

Mozart was one of the most endearing figures ever to have left his mark on history. Though his music exalts the emotions of man, his personal life was characterized by the mundane weaknesses, contradictions and vulnerabilities which are part and parcel of daily existence. He loved and needed the companionship of others – the hundreds of intimately worded letters to parents, sister, wife and friends attest to this.* Naively cheerful, ever ready for a party or for a joke (musical or otherwise, on- or off-color), he was easily taken in, generous, and always convinced his fortunes would improve tomorrow. When tomorrows proved as bleak as yesterdays, he revealed freely his piques, expressed poignantly his sorrows. Hot-tempered and impulsive, he admitted that, if offended, he wanted revenge "with interest." Because he was not worldly wise, not physically prepossessing, nor particularly successful with women – though he was a great flirt and was accused by his wife of "servant gallantries" – the less perceptive tended to underestimate his qualities as musician.

It was, of course, music that ruled Mozart's life, and everything else revolved around it. (Art, literature, the humanities were not of much interest to him.) Whether at any given time he was happy or miserable, cynical or full of hope, his melodies sprang from an inner source that transcended and often contradicted daily existence. And whatever his misjudgments regarding the individuals in his own world, his knowledge of the human spirit was expressed with exquisite clarity where it counted: in the music. That Mozart fully recognized and was not hesitant to admit openly his musical superiority was clear from his early years; this goes far to explain his frequently unsuccessful dealings with the run-of-the-mill musicians and tasteless rulers whom he met. Yes, he would mouth the expected flattering platitudes when necessary, but unfailingly his disdain would make itself felt, musically if not verbally. When pupils proved inept, he would go off with them to play billiards, for mediocrity in music was more than he could stand.

* Mozart's letters, in English translation by Emily Anderson, are delightful reading. There is an unexpectedly earthy – even coarse – tone which is reflective of his typically Salzburg humor.

95

With the few musicians he did not consider inferior, Mozart was capable of warm friendship. Johann Christian Bach, the youngest son of Johann Sebastian, was important to his development as a composer; so was the kindly Italian master Giambattista Martini. But the only one before whom Mozart bowed was Franz Joseph Haydn, to whom he dedicated six string quartets: "I send my six sons to you, most celebrated and very dear friend. Please receive them kindly, and be to them a father and guide and friend." Haydn, in turn, was one who fully recognized Mozart's genius, writing to Leopold: "I tell you before God as an honest man, your son is the greatest composer I know personally or by reputation."

Haydn had a younger brother, Michael, also a musician, who was a Salzburg resident. As director of the archiepiscopal orchestra and later concertmaster and organist at the Cathedral, he was highly esteemed in town. A learned, forceful composer, especially of church music, he had, however, little to teach Mozart, and the latter's family tended to look down on him for his peasant ways and his fondness for beer and wine. Still, Wolfgang liked him and, according to a Haydn student, completed for him a commissioned series of duos which Haydn was too ill to do himself.

One of the mysteries of Mozart's life is how he managed to die a pauper. That he, along with Constanze, was a poor business manager and a spendthrift are well known. Money went on clothes, entertainment, to beggars, in countless moves (the couple changed residence in Vienna ten times in as many years). And on more than one occasion he was woefully underpaid or not paid at all for works composed. Furthermore, the theory and law of copyright were not yet in existence, so the continued success of a composition did not result in coins in his pocket. Still, Mozart did at times earn substantial sums of money. What happened to it all?

In 1977 a German historian named Uwe Kramer wrote an article claiming that Mozart died a pauper because he lost a fortune in obsessive billiard and card playing. (Kramer estimated that from 1783 to 1786 he earned 10,000 gulden a year, the equivalent today of $ 108,000 for concerts alone). This article created a great stir, particularly since its findings were not implausible in terms of Mozart's character. Some musicologists, however, including Harold Schoenberg, dismiss the theory as being based on gossip and unreliable sources. The mystery of Mozart and his money may well remain unsolved.

Rarely do the opinions of one's contemporaries agree with those of future generations. Music, like all the arts, is replete with examples of audiences and musicians scoffing at, misunderstanding, or, worse, neglecting the works of those destined to be considered great by posterity. In the cases of those composers who introduce a great deal that is novel and experimental in their music, it is easy to understand negative audience reaction. With Mozart, it is rather a case of the opposite. Professor Paul Schilhawsky, who was vice-chancellor of the Salzburg Music Academy "Mozarteum", feels the very conformity to accepted forms in many of his works was what fooled the less perceptive. "It is what Mozart did within these forms and with so few notes that was so special," says Schilhawsky. "His work seemed not to be as different from that of his contemporaries as it actually was."

In any case, immediately after Mozart's death, his influence began to be felt all over Europe, particularly as his compositions became available. True, an occasional anti-Mozart person continued to be heard, one fortunately anonymous critic responding to an enthusiastic description of *Don Giovanni* the year after his death with these words: "... I do not know any well grounded connoisseur of art who considers him to be a correct, not to say finished, artist." And true, the 19th century Romantic period which followed though it admired him greatly, also misunderstood him. ("He was called the Raphael of music and was considered an elegant, dainty rococo composer who just happened to have composed *Don Giovanni,*" writes Schoenberg.) But giants of the time like Beethoven, Schubert, Chopin and Brahms, recognizing the power and humanity of his music, were profoundly influenced by Mozart.

In our own century worthy attempts have been made to perform Mozart's works in the spirit and even utilizing the instruments of his time. With this has come increasing reverence for his genius. Hardly a generation has failed to find something new in the music of Wolfgang Amadeus Mozart, or to wonder at a seemingly simple phrase whose effect is so tremendous as to defy analysis. Turning again to Einstein: "Mozart's music which, to many of his contemporaries, seemed to have the brittleness of clay, has long since been transformed into gold, gleaming in the light, though it takes on a different luster for each new generation."

The city of Salzburg began to stir with a vague awareness of its forgotten master early in the 19th century. The first biography, published in 1828, was closely connected with Salzburg, for it was written by a resident, Constanze Mozart's second husband, the Danish Councillor of State, Georg Nikolaus von Nissen. (Constanze herself began to exploit her first husband's name after his death, recognizing belatedly his musical worth and the practical benefits that might derive from it.)

Von Nissen's book, admiring though it was, did not shed many musical insights, but it did give some intriguing information, for example, on Mozart's unimposing appearance: "His head was somewhat large in comparison to his body; the body itself and his hands and feet were well proportioned, a fact of which he was rather vain. His nose was handsome only as long as he was thin. After his marriage the size of his nose was conspicuous."

By 1842 Mozart had become an important enough figure in local eyes so that a bronze statue was erected in his honor on what is now Mozartplatz. Designed by the Munich sculptor Ludwig von Schwanthaler, it was brought to Salzburg by wagon and unveiled in the presence of Mozart's two sons Karl and Wolfgang, Jr.; the latter conducted a Festival Cantata he had composed for the occasion. (Their mother had died six months before.) The larger-than-life but otherwise unimpressive statue has Mozart draped in a mantle, holding a page of music and a copybook.

The Schwanthaler statue was joined some four decades later by a bust of the master placed up on the Kapuzinerberg. Modelled by Edmund Heller of Vienna, it has chiselled upon its base this phrase: "Great when young, belatedly appreciated, never equalled." Actually, the most imaginative of the Mozart-related statues is a more modern work, by the Salzburg sculptress Hilde Heger. This is a fountain above which stands Papageno, the birdcatcher in *The Magic Flute*. Located in a square of the same name (Papagenoplatz), it was commissioned by the municipality after World War II as "a joyous allegory of Mother Nature."

The most important single incentive to the study of Mozart was the formation in 1870 of the International Mozarteum Foundation from an earlier musical association; its main purpose was to be the performance and propagation of Mozart's music. Early on, the Foundation established the Hochschule (college) "Mozarteum". By 1914 the Foundation had its own home in the Schwarzstrasse, next to the Mirabell Gardens. Designed by the Munich architect Richard Berndl, the building became headquarters for the Hochschule, which now has a year-round program and is a leading center for the study of the performing arts, including conducting and theater. The winter program is an intense and long one (eight years for instrumentalists, six for singers), while the summer studies are a counterpart to the festival, utilizing the teaching expertise of performing artists in master classes. Both programs attract students from around the world. The most popular branch of the school is, however, not in the area of performance but education: The Mozarteum's Orff Institute, world headquarters for a system of music education developed by contemporary composer Carl Orff.

Also in the Schwarzstrasse building, the International Mozarteum Foundation has set up a library with 35,000 books, 1500 of these concerning Mozart. In honor of the composer's 200th birthday, the Foundation began a new edition of his works which will total 110 volumes and is expected to be completed in the mid 1980s.* The Foundation's archives contain hundreds of original letters by Wolfgang and Leopold. Of the former, the earliest was written by the composer as a young boy touring in Italy; it was penned in Italian (he also knew English and French) and was addressed to his sister Nannerl. The last, dated only months before his death, went to his wife, then on a spa holiday.

The Mozarteum has two concert halls, the larger one featuring a fine Arco organ. Public performances are given both by students and the Mozarteum's own professional orchestra founded by Moravian-born Joseph Hummel, first director of the Hochschule; presently it is under the baton of Leopold Hager and in 1981 the German Ralf Weikert takes over as principal conductor. Tours of the Mozarteum in summer include an organ concert and a look into the back garden where there stands the restored one-room summer house where Mozart allegedly wrote *The Magic Flute;* it was moved from its original location in Vienna. In front of this cottage on fair summer evenings, the popular Mozart Serenades take place by candlelight.

The International Mozarteum Foundation is responsible for the care and unkeep of the city's leading Mozart monuments and buildings. Of these the most important is his birthplace at Getreidegasse 9. Mozart's family rented the third floor of this 15th century house,

---

* This research is yielding some surprising finds: e.g., that the symphony listed by Köchel as 45A (the Old Lambach Symphony) is not by Wolfgang after, all but by Leopold!

and he was born in the central of their three rooms, overlooking the courtyard. Among its most valuable exhibits are Mozart's clavichord which he used while composing, the grand piano made in Vienna and preferred by him to all others for performance, and the child's size violin.* Also here is the letter sent by Mozart to the Abbé Bullinger about his mother's sudden death in Paris: "Mourn with me, my friend: This has been the saddest day of my life ..." (He could not bear to break the news directly to his father.) Several family portraits are displayed, and the lower floors feature dioramas of Mozart operas as staged in his own time and later.

In 1773 the Mozart family moved to larger quarters on the first floor of Hannibalplatz 8 (now Makartplatz), known as the Dancing Master's Hall after the former owner. Here they were able to hold small concerts. After leaving the archbishop's service, Mozart stayed in the house only once – in 1783 – when he brought his wife for a visit. Most of the building was destroyed in an air raid during World War II, and of the family's apartment only the music room remained. That room has now been restored to its original appearance, and concerts are held here.

There are numerous other locales in Salzburg which are of interest to the student of Mozart. He was christened at the Cathedral. At the University he acted in plays, and one of his operas, composed at the age of eleven, was staged here in the Aula Academica. In the wine cellar of St. Peter's monastery Leopold used to sing from his own quartets. In the Residenz Wolfgang conducted his own works, and in the Mirabell Palace he performed with Leopold and Nannerl. In St. Peter's Church he supposedly conducted the first performance of his C Minor Mass with his wife singing the soprano solo. The Mozart family paid frequent visits to the elegant country house

---

* Remarkable stories about the child Mozart are many, one of which concerns this very violin. When Wolfgang was four years old, a court musician, Andreas Schatner, came to play trios at the Mozart home with Leopold and a third musician. Wolfgang begged to be allowed to play the violin part, but Leopold refused since his son had never had a lesson on the instrument. Schatner, seeing how upset the child was by his father's rebuff, intervened on Wolfgang's behalf. The boy was then permitted to try the second violin part with Schatner. Years later, the latter recalled this incident in a letter to Nannerl: "I soon noticed with astonishment that I was quite superfluous. I quietly put my violin down and looked at your Papa; tears of wonder and comfort ran down his cheeks at this scene."

Robinighof. Constanze lived with her second husband in a house on the Old Market Place. She and von Nissen are buried at St. Sebastian's as is Leopold, and Nannerl's grave is at St. Peter's. One notion, long accepted as fact but now disclaimed, is that Mozart wrote his Coronation Mass for the twin-towered pilgrimage church of Maria Plain to the north of Salzburg.

Of course the most significant of Salzburg's monuments to Mozart are the performances of his work, and these are everywhere and in every season. While the summer festival is inextricably tied to the music of Mozart, the most concentrated presentation of his works occurs each year during Mozart Week *(Mozartwoche)* at the end of January around his birthday.

Just a few miles outside of Salzburg in the village of Grödig, there is a chocolate factory called Mirabell. Its specialty, created in 1890 by a confectioner named Paul Fürst, is a delectable round goody made of pistachio-flavored marzipan, rolled in nougat cream and then dipped in a rich bitter chocolate. These fattening and expensive delights are known as Mozartkugeln (Mozart Balls), and each is covered in a shiny tin foil wrapper sporting a full-color likeness of Wolfgang Amadeus Mozart himself. So popular are the chocolate balls (150,000 are produced each day) that many firms have tried to imitate them. Mirabell protects itself by patenting the round shape and adding the word *Echte* to its name ("*Real* Mozart Balls"). This has not stopped the competition; one factory puts out a chocolate with a flat bottom and another more enterprising gentleman has turned the *Kugel* into a *Würfel,* or cube.

But the Mirabell factory reigns supreme. It also manufactures a kind of companion piece, pancake-shaped wafers known as *Mozart Tortelettes* which have gooier insides and feature characters from Mozart's operas on the wrappers. Together these candies make their way to the leading sweetshops in Salzburg, where they form the focal point of many a display window. It's a pretty picture with hundreds of chocolates placed around a large, serene portrait of the composer, dressed as he is in the paper foil: carefully curled silver locks tied back with a black velvet bow, reddened, smiling lips, white ruffled shirt, royal blue vest and brilliant red jacket edged in gold. It is, in fact, a lot prettier than Mozart's life.

And chocolates are only one item. As an economic factor, Mozart is hard to beat in Salzburg. Dixie cups, buses, hotels, movie houses, even foot baths, they all have been named after him. It amounts to adulation; some would call it exploitation. The fact is, in Salzburg Wolfgang Amadeus Mozart has been raised from ignominy to legend – this one, for instance: God sits on his throne in the kingdom of heaven. Surrounding him are the greats of history – Shakespeare, Michelangelo and, naturally, Mozart, among them. But only Mozart has a favored spot: seated upon God's knee.

One can hardly escape the irony of Mozart's least favorite city having become a mecca for his admirers. But modern Salzburg is not responsible for the musical judgments of the past. As for the gimmicks, even those of questionable taste, they are mere frills. What is important is that today in Salzburg, Mozart's music is being played – played well and often and joyously.

CHAPTER SEVEN
THE GLORIOUS SUMMER FESTIVAL

It was only natural that Salzburg would become the home of a great festival. The city was itself a stage, planned with dash and daring, upon which had grown a rich artistic tradition of opera, theater and church music. That tradition reached its zenith in the works of Wolfgang Amadeus Mozart.

From the mid 19th century on there were attempts in Salzburg to initiate a regular cultural event concentrating on Mozart's works. As the musical world's awareness of his genius grew, so did plans for that festival. The fall of the Austro-Hungarian Monarchy at the end of World War I delayed the festival's onset but at the same time gave it more impetus, for in the face of the senseless slaughter and cruelty it seemed that only the arts – especially music and, above all, Mozart's music – could help heal the wounds and restore man's hope.

Before the war was even over, there began a public appeal to fund the Salzburg Festival. This proclamation was issued: "Mist surrounds the world and there seems to be no end to the cruelest of wars. Nobody knows what the next hour is going to bring. All the same, we will dare to express the thought of a Salzburg festival devoted to peace, art and joy. We call upon those who believe in the might of art, upon those who believe the works and values of art to be the only stable things in the eternal changes of time, to join us and to help us establish a refuge in the name of Mozart where art lovers of all countries may unite in festive delight once the dark clouds of this world catastrophe have passed."

There were many individuals with vision and a spirit of adventure who made the idea become reality but three names stand out. Max Reinhardt, Hugo von Hofmannsthal and Richard Strauss, brilliant artists, very dissimilar in personality, brought their own unique gifts to this ambitious venture.

Reinhardt was a theater director of immense skill and with a magician's touch. Born near Vienna in Baden in 1873 to a Jewish family which hoped he would become a banker, he was from the beginning more attracted to the stage. His first youthful success was as an actor, specializing in elderly character roles, in the municipal theater of Salzburg. There he was discovered by the famed director Otto Brahm who hired him on the spot for his own Berlin company, the Deutsches Theater ("German Theater"). Brahm might not have been so anxious to have the actor if he had realized that in time Reinhardt would succeed him as director of that very theater.

Reinhardt's professional ideas proved to be very different from those of Brahm. Whereas the latter sought a naturalistic, muted, objective effect, with the actor always subordinate to the words of the play, Reinhardt emphasized whatever aspect of the production he felt would best bring the play to life. Hence his stagings were full of color, music and spectacle. His was a truly baroque approach, one that was to prove well suited to Salzburg. Gisela Prossnitz, head of the Salzburg institute that today honors Reinhardt through research and exhibitions states: "He made the theater, which had been the domain of the spoken word, once more the common property of the arts."

Reinhardt had his Berlin company perform not only in customary theaters but in circus arenas lavishly set and with enormous casts, in cabarets, in intimate houses with the actors numbering only four or five, in the open air with the green grass as his stage. He travelled the continent, and eventually America, with his productions, achieving renown for a large variety of interpretations including Sophocles, Shakespeare, Molière, Ibsen and Wilde. Hugo von Hofmannsthal wrote, "He attacks each fresh piece of work as a child attacks a new toy, with the absolute unconcern of a visionary who, before he enchants his audience, wishes first to enchant himself."

A small, stocky man with twinkling blue eyes and wavy hair, Reinhardt was beloved by his actors, for, being an actor himself, he was able to draw out of them their own deepest comprehension of a role. His boundless energy and imagination were balanced by a rigorous attention to detail and a gift for organization. Indeed, Reinhardt had precisely the qualities to utilize fully the physical and artistic potential of Salzburg which he had appreciated since his first theater season there as a young actor barely out of his teens. ("Salzburg," he was to say years later, "is the home of my heart.")

The town had yet another facet to its attraction, for here Reinhardt felt the Austro-Bavarian theater to be most strongly rooted. In its enjoyment of play and spectacle, its light, deft touch, this was a vastly different theater from the Berlin school which had taught him other things: restraint, economy, and a knowledge of the North-German literature.

Reinhardt made the Salzburg Festival the culmination of his life's work, giving up the direction of the Deutsches Theater so that he could devote himself to it. He wanted the Festival to be as free as possible from commercial considerations, in the early years taking no money for his efforts as director and asking the same of his actors. Admittedly, Reinhardt was far from impoverished. In 1918 he bought Schloss Leopoldskron, Leopold Firmian's old home, which during Reinhardt's time there knew a glamorous life unmatched before or since.

The individual who was to work most closely with him in the Festival's dramatic offerings and who determined the basic philosophy of the new venture, was Austria's renowned poet, dramatist, essayist, and one of the finest librettists in operatic history: Hugo von Hofmannsthal. Born in Vienna in 1874 to a patrician family of varied origin (Austrian, Swabian, Lombard, and with a Jewish grandfather on one side), he studied law, languages and literature, becoming a widely learned man of culture. Described as darkly Italian in appearance, Hofmannsthal was proud and rather snobbish, withdrawn, sensitive and – until the inflation of 1920 – wealthy. Despite this worldly fame and fortune, he was given to morbid self-doubts and brooding melancholia. Possessing a keen knowledge of and respect for the past, Hofmannsthal was deeply troubled by the moral decline brought about by World War I. Yet he showed strength and enthusiasm for the project of turning the small city of Salzburg (population 40,000) to the service of the arts, utilizing his cultural and political knowledge toward the goal of restoring morality through art. Taking old plays which revealed a similar concern, he adapted them with new vision for his own time and infused them with an elegance born of his rich, flowing language.

Hofmannsthal was aware that the Festival audiences would most probably be an amalgam of several groups – established wealth and nouveaux riches, stage giants and stagestruck, society kings, financiers, literati and hangers-on. Vital to this mix, in his view, were the area's country folk, a group that would only be at home through the presentation of dramatic fare that sprang from its own roots. Like Reinhardt, he was much interested in the folk theater of the Salzburg region.

Hofmannsthal's work as librettist brought glory of another sort upon the Festival and, indeed, continues to do so. As the artist who collaborated with composer Richard Strauss in one of the longest partnerships known to music, he produced the texts for some of Strauss' finest operas, including the savage story of *Elektra* and the comic masterpiece *Der Rosenkavalier*. Strauss biographer George

Marek writes, "Hofmannsthal's Austrian refinement balanced Strauss' strong and occasionally tasteless German genius."

Not the least of Hofmannsthal's contributions to the Salzburg Festival was the formula he devised for it: Mozart's music as the focal point, a fringe of theater from classical to contemporary, and operas from Gluck to his own collaborator Strauss. The recipe was sound and, despite dramatically changing times and tastes, has been successful to this day.

With Strauss we come to the last of the major Festival founders*. He was a man of almost irreconcilable contradictions. Reserved, gentlemanly, industrious, a punctilious businessman, he revealed in his tone poems and operas a passion, daring and psychological insights that were missing from his relations with others. Münich-born in 1864 to a musican father whose idols were Mozart and Beethoven, Strauss eventually took as his own god the man whose music his father most detested: Richard Wagner. Strauss, Sr. was also anti-Semitic, a trait which doubtless contributed to the son's ambivalent feelings about his own Jewish musican friends.

Richard Strauss was a man whom few knew intimately. Though he collaborated with Hofmannsthal for 25 years and said of their relationship, "we were made for each other," the two continued through all that time to address each other using formal *Sie* ("you") in correspondence; they were partners, not companions.

Reinhardt was far from incidental to this collaboration. It was he who inspired Strauss, through a brilliant staging of the Oscar Wilde play *Salome* about an erotic, demented princess, to compose an opera on the same subject. The result was a shocking, almost unbearably tense work that places enormous demands on both singers and audience but, when well performed, is unsurpassed on the operatic stage for sheer power. At Strauss' request, Reinhardt directed the world premiere of this and several of his other operas, fully recognized by the composer and by Hofmannsthal as the brilliant director he was.

Strauss had another career that proved very useful to the new project: he was a noted conductor. In fact, he had led the 1906 Salzburg concert commemorating the 150th anniversary of Mozart's birth.

---

* Many others of importance were involved, including conductor Franz Schalk, stage designer Alfred Roller, and city councillor Friedrich Gehmacher.

The Salzburg Festival was to open in 1919 but, due to an inadequate food supply, the inaugural performance was delayed until August 1920. Chosen for the long awaited occasion was a Hofmannsthal adaptation of the medieval morality play *Jedermann (Everyman)*, subtitled "The Play of the Rich Man's Death." First published in London in 1490, *Jedermann* was a natural for Hofmannsthal, who retained the basic story while enhancing it with a finely honed, simple but sophisticated German text. His adaptation, as staged by Reinhardt, had been performed earlier in Berlin without great success, but in Salzburg it succeeded wildly and became – without either Hofmannsthal or Reinhardt so intending – the very symbol of the Festival.

The story could not have been more simple: a rich, middle-aged man, unconcerned with matters other than his own wealth, mistress and the new pleasure palace he is building, refuses to give up his godless life despite his aged mother's sadness or the pathetic case of a poor debtor going to jail because of him. He puts on a splendid feast at which, suddenly, Death appears, calling him to his judgment. *Everyman*, fearful, begs time, but all he can have is one hour. Allowed company on this bleak journey, he is, however, deserted by all his erstwhile friends: his cousins, manservant, mistress, even his gold. The figures Good Works and Faith come to help him repent and save his soul, Good Works needing crutches for support, as *Everyman* had done no good works in his life to strengthen her. With their help he regains his lost soul, successfully repulsing the Devil who has come to claim him. Dressed in pure white, his face shining with glory, *Everyman* is lowered into his grave, angels singing of his redemption.

It is impossible to grasp fully the power of this play without seeing it – and it can be seen today much as it was in 1920. For the presentation Reinhardt received permission from the archbishop to stage it outside on the enclosed Cathedral square on the steps of the Cathedral. An audience of 5,000 strong sat spellbound, traffic was stopped, and at the end, many – including the archbishop and the Cathedral Chapter who were in the first row of the audience – wept. As for the country folk, they were so moved that the next year they paid *Jedermann* the ultimate compliment: they staged it in their own villages and even toured with it in dialect.

The old story, new poetry, lavish settings and superb acting had combined with the stunning theatrical effects to make of the very first Salzburg Festival performance a veritable *tour de force*. There was no end to the thrilling moments: thunder reverberating from inside the Cathedral as God spoke, *Everyman* called to his judgment by invisible ghostly voices emanating from the church steeples and even the fortress high up on the hill, the red devil leaping from the spectators' benches, and Mammon *(Everyman's* riches) springing up from a huge chest, bald, half naked and dripping with coins. Even the time of day played its part, for the prologue took place in the warm light of late afternoon, while by the finale a dying sun gleamed upon the crosses at the pinnacle of the Cathedral's twin towers. *Everyman* was baroque to the core and, like true baroque works of art, overwhelmed the senses.

The man who acted *Everyman* in the early years was Alexander Moissi, an artist of aristocratic, slender grace and a fine voice. Reinhardt's second wife, the actress Helene Thimig, took on the role of Good Works. (Thimig was active in the play's production even after Reinhardt's death many years later.) Those who saw her in that compared her to a Gothic madonna. The part of Death was taken by Werner Krauss, who left his mark in a droll incidental way: since the actors were not paid during the first years of the Festival, they received souvenirs instead. Krauss was quite clear about what he wanted – a pair of *Lederhosen* (leather shorts).

By 1922 another of Hofmannsthal's so-called festival dramas had been produced: *Das Salzburger grosse Welttheater (The Salzburg Great World Theater)*. Again an adaptation, this was originally the work of 17th century Spanish playright Calderón. Reinhardt chose a different but similarly inspired setting: Fischer von Erlach's Collegiate Church. People sat for almost three hours without one intermission to watch this allegorical work that deals with the world as a stage upon which men (the King, Rich Man, Beauty, the Farmer, the Beggar, etc.) act the parts assigned them by God. For the production Alfred Roller, gifted stage designer from the Vienna State Opera, built a simple platform which served as stage in front of the high altar; he draped the altar in scarlet, the ecclesiastical color for martyrs. The scene in which the various people who make up the world theater faced Death was breathtaking. Death had been standing motionless as a statue upon the high altar. Sliding down by means of an invisible ladder, the slender figure dressed in scarlet and a black Spanish cape beat with bone drumsticks upon an unseen drum affixed to his body, while in the organ loft hidden gongs and kettledrums sounded.

A third festival drama was seen in Salzburg in 1925: *The Miracle*.

This wordless pantomime with music had been adapted by Carl Vollmoeller from a play by Maurice Maeterlinck. Staged previously by Reinhardt in New York to audience and critical acclaim, the story is of a nun who, wooed by a prince, leaves the convent, whereupon the figure of the Virgin is reincarnated and takes the erring nun's place. The spiritual, psychic pageant employed the use of orchestra, song, cloister chimes, giant cymbals, and thousands of lights. The setting? Of course, another church. This time it was the Franciscan, whose musty and mysterious nave opens dramatically into the daylight of the choir.

Incidentally, Reinhardt's preference for churches was due to more than just their beauty. The sensuousness of these places of worship, with their candles, organ, incense, the richly robed priests, appealed to him greatly. In such a setting, he felt the highest and most holy was revealed to man.

Theatrical productions were, of course, just one aspect of the Festival. No matter how much *Everyman* appealed to Austrian and German audiences, the founders were cognizant that only the international language of music would bring in the desired international audiences. Besides, Mozart was at the very heart of the Festival concept.

The musical part of the Salzburg Festival was inaugurated in 1922 with performances of four Mozart operas, of which Richard Strauss conducted two. This was only the beginning. The Vienna Philharmonic played his orchestral works and chamber ensembles his *divertimenti.* His C-Minor Mass was presented in the Cathedral, while guests at Leopoldskron were serenaded from the balcony by his chamber works. Finally the Salzburg master had attained his rightful place in the town of his birth. After Mozart came many others. The 1929 performance of Strauss' *Der Rosenkavalier* with the composer at the podium and Salzburg's own Richard Mayr in a leading role was a particularly exciting occasion. Another success of the first decade was Beethoven's opera *Fidelio* with the great German soprano Lotte Lehmann, also under the baton of Strauss.

That other master of German opera, Wagner, was represented by *Tristan and Isolde* with Bruno Walter conducting, but Wagner never established a permanent rule in Salzburg, largely because the Bayreuth Festival exists precisely to glorify his name. Italian operas as exemplified by Verdi have, however, become staples of the repertoire.

In 1929 Hugo von Hofmannsthal died. His son had committed suicide in his parent's home, and on the morning of the funeral the elder Hofmannsthal suffered a heart attack which proved fatal. So deeply was the elder Hofmannsthal mourned in his nature city that it was written of his funeral: "... all the rosebushes of Vienna must have been plucked."

Though this was a great loss to the Festival, Hofmannsthal continued to live through his works. Reinhardt staged many other plays as well, his rendition of Shakespeare's *A Midsummer Night's Dream* being particularly renowned. In 1933 he brought the first part of Goethe's *Faust* to Salzburg. For this remarkable production staged in the Felsenreitschule, the former Summer Riding School which is built into the Mönchsberg mountain, the Tyrolean architect Clemens Holzmeister constructed an entire "Faust City", a multiple stage medieval town with real houses and grass. A tree was transferred from the Mönchsberg to the Felsenreitschule stage where it served, and continues to serve, a unique dramatic and aesthetic function.

The development of the Festival building complex is an interesting story in itself. Churches and squares were fine for certain performances, but with multiplying crowds and many different kinds of productions, additional halls were vital. In the beginning Reinhardt hoped to make Markus Sittikus' old palace Hellbrunn the center of the Festival. The gifted German architect Hans Poelzig was chosen for this project which was to include a great temple-like hall for grand opera and a smaller, more delicate one suited to Mozart, along with workshops, studios, rehearsal halls, terraces, arcades and restaurants. Though the cornerstone was laid, financial restrictions made this plan impossible.

Instead, another – and in the end more original – scheme was developed in an ideally central location. Its nucleus was the royal stables built under Wolf Dietrich and completed later by Fischer von Erlach. With room for 130 horses and contingents, the stables had long since been converted from their onetime princely use to the more undignified one of barracks.

The first festival hall was the work of a local architect, Eduard Hütter, who adapted the Winter Riding School for that purpose. By 1925 work had advanced sufficiently for performances to begin. The hall was enlarged and completed under Holzmeister, creator of "Faust City". The exquisitely colored and noble frescoes by high ranking Austrian artist Anton Faistauer* gave the vestibule a festive character. Holzmeister completely redesigned the theater in the 1930's with new technical equipment, more seats, and a reversal in audience orientation. This was once again – after World War II – to be modified and is known today as the Kleines Festspielhaus (Small Festival Hall).

The adaptation of the Felsenreitschule, with a convertible roof, stage and orchestra pit added, made of this outdoor riding school a second fine hall, the setting for *Faust* and many other memorable productions. It was a natural theater with three tiers of colonnades carved out of the rocky cliff – the same area from which guests of the archbishop used to admire the royal steeds. Lavishly decorated with marble balustrades and baroque ceiling frescoes, the Felsenreitschule remains Salzburg's most unusual theater.

The 1930's until the *Anschluss* in 1938 (annexation by Germany) were probably the brightest in the Salzburg Festival's history. The event was unrivalled in its influence, and to be invited as a participating artist, from singer to stage designer, was a distinct honor. The social headquarters of all this glamour were in Leopoldskron Palace. Quiet by day (when Reinhardt customarily slept), it was alive and aglitter all night with candles and servants dressed in red and gold livery.** Here Reinhardt and his wife entertained, offering their guests caviar and venison, champagne and burgundy. The private theatrical entertainments staged both inside the palace and in the garden theater were legendary. In this milieu, politics and the bleak future of Europe did not loom as real as they were; the beautiful illusion of the arts reigned supreme.

Stefan Zweig's villa up on the Kapuzinerberg was another focal point for august visitors. Viennese-born, affluent, the modest Zweig was a world traveller, poet and essayist, as well as an ardent worker for world peace. He had moved to Salzburg in 1919, finding here men and women of like minds and hopes. These were also the years of critic Hermann Bahr who wrote so lovingly of Salzburg, yet whom Reinhardt treated with what has been described as "reverential distrust."

* well known also for his frescoes at the parish church of Morzg

** According to one oft repeated story, a Wall Street mogul, after being escorted up Leopoldskron's marble staircase, aglow with hundreds of candles, greeted his host with this comment: "What's the matter? Short circuit?"

During the glittering summer months the coffee houses, restaurants and beer gardens were full to the brim. Chewing their rolls, heads buried in newspaper reviews of this performance or that one, the customers virtually inhaled the Festival with their coffee. Already prices were much higher than many residents could afford, and the concièrge at the Goldener Hirsch Hotel was getting rich by selling tickets at black market prices.

Now the country people whom the Festival had sought to involve earlier were being pushed into the background. The distinction between the social classes had become nakedly apparent, and even *Jedermann* couldn't bring them together.

Among the most glorious Festival years – years in which the sense of impending doom gave a measure of poignancy to the event – were those prior to World War II. From 1935 until 1937 Arturo Toscanini came to Salzburg to conduct selected operas; with him were his Cadillac, his chauffeur Emilio, his family and a claque of worshippers. He became the idol of Salzburg and returned the love fervently. Stefan Zweig, who became a friend to the diminutive Italian *maestro* wrote, "I blessed my fate which tied my life to his."

Toscanini was no youngster in the Salzburg years and, at the threshold of his seventieth decade, he decided to retire from directorship of the New York Philharmonic. But his energy was still boundless. Each time he conducted without pay, receiving instead his own choice of artists, as many rehearsals as he wished with the Vienna Philharmonic (they numbered as many as 60), and total control over each performance. The results were electric. Of one *Fidelio* Marek writes: "It was raining that August night in Salzburg, and it was cold. But when the curtain rose on the last scene, the sunshine of the music warmed your skin and you listened in hope to a promise which has not been fulfilled." Another of Toscanini's great interpretations here was Wagner's *Die Meistersinger*, introduced in 1936. For the first time Americans could hear the Festival operas from across the miles, broadcast by NBC.

Toscanini's happiness in Salzburg was short-lived. By the summer of 1937 the handwriting was on the wall: *Anschluss.* Earlier, Toscanini had been an admirer of the Italian dictator Mussolini, but by now he had turned against him and the German *Führer* Hitler with a vengeance, recognizing fully the evil they personified. Toscanini's behavior at that time and later was both highly moral and unusually courageous. A major confrontation with the Nazis occurred on the occasion of the first planned broadcast exchange between the operatic performances of Bayreuth and those of Salzburg. Bruno Walter, a Jew, would not be accepted by German radio, Toscanini learned. In response he vetoed the whole plan. The Nazis retaliated: German singers were forbidden to sing in Salzburg. This order fell on at least some deaf ears. Lotte Lehmann, for one, a "pure" Aryan, a German and one of the greatest singers of all time, had declared that under no circumstances would she sing for the *Reich*.

The dress rehearsal of *Die Meistersinger* that year is one of those occasions that witnesses have never forgotten. Marcia Davenport, a novelist who was present, recalled years later that: "It was a performance in which every participant was genuinely inspired. It went without a flaw from beginning to end... When the curtain fell on the finale, and then went up again as curtains do at rehearsals for technical reasons, there stood the entire company on stage, every one of them in tears. Maestro himself stood motionless in his place with his right hand covering his eyes. I do not know what may have lain in the hearts of those singers and musicians, but I have often sensed that for some of them this was their defiant defence of their German heritage in the face of the obscenities across the frontier."

Toscanini decided that the Summer of 1937 would be his last in Salzburg. Bruno Walter wrote him, pleading that he rethink his cancellation: "You know better than I ... that Salzburg is perhaps the last nonpolitical spot left where art still has a roof over its head." Toscanini answered by begging Walter to get out himself. His own exit from Italy to the U.S. was temporarily halted when Mussolini, supposedly at the instigation of Hitler, confiscated his passport. But he did make it back to New York, where his home became a headquarters of the musical world's resistance to Fascism and Nazism. On March 4, 1938 Toscanini was to have held a benefit concert at Carnegie Hall for the Salzburg Festival, but the month before he changed the beneficiaries to unemployed and indigent musicians. Anyone who disagreed with this action could have his money refunded; not one ticket was returned.

Richard Strauss took over some of Toscanini's Salzburg performances. Strauss' own position was that of a fence-walker. He both accepted honors and favors from the Third *Reich* and, at the same time, endangered himself by maintaining his Jewish ties – albeit generally for reasons of art rather than morality. He tried, for instance, to protect his new collaborator, the Jewish Stefan Zweig through the Propaganda minister Goebbels, but Zweig wanted no

113

favors from the Nazis. He left Austria, tried to make a new life abroad, and ended up committing suicide in Brazil. Reinhardt was luckier, moving to the U.S. where he achieved some renown in Hollywood and New York before his death at the age of 70.* Hofmannsthal who, because of his Jewish grandfather, had been classified as "non-Aryan," was now reclassified as "Jewish", but since he had died several years earlier performances of his works were not disallowed.

In this way Adolf Hitler's Nazism destroyed that special magic that had been wrought by people joined in the arts, whatever their political, ethnic, or national background. Taking over the Festival program and buildings, he determined on replacing the "degenerate modern art" with classic "Aryan" work. On visiting the Kleines Festspielhaus, his expression betrayed displeasure with the Faistauer frescoes, whereupon one of his adjutants gave the order for them to be removed. (Fortunately a painter/restorer salvaged most of them, and after the war they were reinstalled.)

Richard Strauss had the good fortune to meet an intelligent musician, conductor Clemens Krauss, who spurred him on to some late success. A flamboyant and demanding conductor, Krauss, too, had been willing to serve the Reich; in 1941 he was rewarded with the Festival's artistic leadership. Krauss convinced Strauss to release for performance his new opera *Die Liebe der Danae*. The première was to be in 1944 in honor of the composer's 80th birthday.

This was the height of the war. The Allies had entered Rome and landed on the beaches of Normandy. All theater festivals had been suspended by the *Reich,* though Salzburg's was permitted to continue in truncated form. But August 16, 1944 marked its close. It was the final dress rehearsal of *Danae* to which an audience of special guests had been invited, and Strauss was visibly moved. At the end he laid down his baton, saying in a tearful voice to the members of the Vienna Philharmonic: "Perhaps we shall see each other in a better world."

An empty desolation fell upon the festival halls, the terrible noise of bombs replacing Mozart's melodies. But when the war was finally over, Austria's remarkable courage revealed itself through a

---

* The newest work on Reinhardt to appear in English is the translation of a biography, *The Genius,* by his son Gottfried Reinhardt; it was published by Knopf in 1979.

resurgence of that which was dearest: music. Vienna pulled itself up from under the rubble and despair and so did Salzburg. The Festival was once again in business by 1947, the first summer being launched under the patronage of the U.S. Army. On the program were Mozart's *Il Seraglio* and Hofmannsthal's bleak lyrical drama *Der Tor und der Tod (The Fool and Death)*, about a man who lacks the courage in life to form commitments or loyalties and only in death realizes that he has never made real contact with anyone.

Jedermann returned a year later, its impact frighteningly intense. Strauss' *Danae* belatedly made it to the stage in 1952, proving to be a ponderous work which, however, was given a fine performance under Krauss. Bernhard Paumgartner, head of the Mozarteum and later Festival president, began the Mozart matinees and serenades – perhaps reflecting the most characteristic Salzburg aura of all the festival events. The Mozart and Strauss specialist Karl Böhm, who had first conducted in Salzburg in 1938, returned; in the courtyard of the Residenz he led the lighthearted opera *Così fan tutte*.

Important architectural work was carried out as well, resulting in a single Festival complex 150 yards long. The old house of Hütter and Holzmeister was adapted to its present form by architects Hans Hofmann and Erich Engels. Though known as the "Small Festival Hall," it is far from small, seating 1343. A brand new Grosses Festspielhaus (Large Festival Hall) was built alongside it in 1956–60 by Holzmeister, who saved the monumental old Fischer von Erlach façade and created the huge backstage area by blasting into the rock of the Mönchsberg. An audience of 2371 can be accommodated in this house. Its stage, which can be extended to a width of 90 feet, is the largest in Europe with the exception of the Bolshoi Theater in Moscow – something that stage directors have fully exploited in recent years for the mass scenes in operas such as *Aida, Don Carlos* and *Fidelio*. The decor is distinctly contemporary, with a notable tapestry by Oskar Kokoschka ("Love and Psyche"). The floor mosaics are of Untersberg marble with inlaid heads and shoes of horses. As for the Felsenreitschule, it was given a much needed new retractable roof which can be drawn back on warm summer evenings, creating an open-air atmosphere, or remain closed when the weather is less benign.*

---

* The visitor is well advised to take advantage of the free summer tours of Salzburg's festival halls; these provide a much more comprehensive understanding than can be obtained at a performance. However during the festival itself no tours take place.

Almost half a century ago Arturo Toscanini befriended a young musician at the Salzburg Festival. He was locally born, a doctor's son, had been a student at the Mozarteum, and was doing odd jobs around the Festspielhaus while off from his regular position as artistic director of a third-rate municipal opera house. His name was Herbert von Karajan.

Today Karajan is the Festival's superstar, idol, king and headline maker. As permanent conductor of the Berlin Philharmonic – an orchestra which he restored to its pre-war glory and refers to as "an extension of my arms" – he and it perform here regularly. He also guest conducts the Vienna Philharmonic which, having been the first orchestra to appear at the Festival, is regarded with much sentiment. Now leading a rather less hectic life than he did as a younger man (he used to be dubbed "general music director of Europe"), Karajan still finds new ways to drum up world publicity. Recently he patched up a longtime feud with the Vienna State Opera, returning to its podium with suitable fanfare and audience hysteria.

In Salzburg however, Karajan is much more than a busy and admired conductor. A former artistic director of the Festival, he continues from behind the scenes as a member of the governing board to dominate and influence decisions regarding programs and artists. Whenever he appears personally, his name automatically becomes more important than that of the singers, the orchestra, even the work performed. Karajan's photograph is everywhere: it stares at you from inside record shops, on billboards, in newspapers, with a ubiquity equalled only by Mozart's smiling image upon chocolate wrappers.

The smallish, icily handsome maestro with the blue-green eyes, the waving grey hair brushed high and the aristocratic mien is of as much interest locally for his private life as his public doings. Residents follow every bit of news about his chic French wife Eliette, their villa in Anif just south of Salzburg, his quarrels with Austrian officialdom and other musicians, his expensive toys (sports cars, planes, etc.) and when he was younger his daredevil feats.

In personality Karajan is cool, reserved, proud and vain. His favored musicans are deeply loyal, and he has a goodly supply of charm for use when he wants to achieve his characteristically exacting standards. One aspect of Karajan's career has not engendered affection in many quarters and accounts for a continuing unpopularity in the U.S. and England: the fact that he was supported by the Nazi party. This past he has at times defended, saying (like Strauss)

116

that he paid no attention to anything but music; other times he has admitted to a ruthless streak which put career before scruples.

On the podium Karajan has few peers and, like all great conductors, he is unique. His technique is polished, elegant and masterfully controlled; his hands are extraordinarily flexible and capable of exceedingly supple gestures. He is no gyrator on stage; each gesture has a musical meaning. The result of all this is silken, dazzling, clean, classically correct orchestral interpretation. Matched with this is a highly individual approach to staging which is sometimes acclaimed, at other times ridiculed. A Karajan production of *Fidelio* in the Felsenreitschule was so breathtaking in dramatic impact that many compared it to Reinhardt's productions.

Martin Mayer wrote in a New York Times Magazine profile of this musican: "What has made Karajan so huge a phenomenon on the postwar musical scene... is neither his musicianship nor his intelligence; it is the fact that all his abilities are constantly at the service of an irradiating theatrical projection."

Karajan's power in Salzburg can be seen clearly in the satellite festivals that he has built up around the summer event and of which he is literally owner. The bigger is the Easter Festival, founded in 1967. This is a week-plus long series of concerts and operas which was initially to be devoted to works by Wagner, but Verdi, Mahler and Bruckner have also been well represented; it is organized at great cost with significant help from the city, *Land* and private sponsors. Karajan utilizes the money he receives entirely for the performances, but derives his own very substantial income from recordings made here with his own Berlin Philharmonic. He is the producer, stage director, conductor, record and film maker. It is almost impossible to obtain tickets for this expensive event; the tickets are sold out before most people have even seen the advance program. To make it more difficult, most tickets are not sold singly but as a series of three performances.

The other Karajan-Berlin Philharmonic event is the Whitsuntide Festival which takes place in May or June. Usually three days in length and consisting purely of orchestral works, this series on occasion has featured symphonies by Mahler. Tickets, once again, are hard to come by and sold through subscription.

Though one may sometimes think otherwise, there are other conductors at the Salzburg Festival besides Herbert von Karajan. In fact, the number of *maestri* in a given season is usually generous, and it is both instructive and fascinating to compare the various conductors as they take the lead of the various orchestras. Traditionally, the Vienna Philharmonic, recognized for its cultured, noble tone, opens and dominates the orchestral series. The London Symphony Orchestra has appeared on three occasions, the Israel Philharmonic played as recently as in 1979, and the Berlin Philharmonic is no longer counted as a guest orchestra but appears regularly at the end of the season. Salzburg's own Mozarteum Orchestra under Leopold Hager is far more than a local group, having performed, for instance, at the Metropolitan Opera in New York. On the podium have stood Leonard Bernstein, James Levine, André Previn, Zubin Mehta, Claudo Abbado, Riccardo Muti, Karl Böhm and Seiji Ozawa, to name just a few.

Mozart matinees and serenades, intimate and ever appealing, continue each year. Various chamber groups are invited to perform, the Solisti Veneti from Italy being a favorite. There is hardly a top singer or instrumentalist who has not done recital work in Salzburg, from baritone Dietrich Fischer-Dieskau to soprano Leontyne Price, from pianist Sviatoslav Richter to cellist Mstislav Rostropovich.

Every year there are one or two Mozart operas along with such composers as Verdi and Strauss. Recently acclaimed was the first production in Salzburg of the latter's *Salome* with a Karajan-coached singer, Hildegard Behrens, in the leading role. In 1978 the festival staged a new production of Strauss' *Der Rosenkavalier*, about which the New York Times said rather snidely that this was "the epitome of the festival itself... safe, solid and sumptuous." It had "one more of everything than most productions can afford... [including] a dog handler with four fluffy canines."

In the continuing attempt to revive works of the long past, the festival management brought the Italian opera *Il Sant' Alessio* by Landi (1632) to the stage. Another tradition is that of church music; the 1200th birthday of the Cathedral was celebrated with masses that spanned the centuries, from Palestrina to Penderecki. The ORF (Austrian Radio) Symphony Orchestra has made a noble – if not always successful – attempt to bring new works to Salzburg. Theater continues its long Salzburg connection at the Landestheater (Provincial Theater), built in 1893–94 by the well known theater architects Helmer and Fellner. Given here are classical and contemporary works, some of which are quite adventurous. A German version of the monologue *Clarence Darrow for the Defense* by Irving Stone starred Curd Jürgens. Thomas Bernhard, winner of the

118

Austrian State Prize for the novel, has been represented at Salzburg by several plays, reminiscent in their despair of another important literary figure linked with the city, its brilliant native poet Georg Trakl. Contemporary playwright Rolf Hochhuth has also written for the Festival; his *Death of a Hunter,* which dealt with the suicide of Ernest Hemingway, also featured Jürgens. The same actor played *Everyman* for some years, his co-star being Senta Berger. In 1978 Maximilian Schell took over the role of *Everyman.*

Yes, *Jedermann* is still around, still exciting, still relevant, still sold out. Crowds gather about an hour before each performance hoping to buy inexpensive standing room tickets, available only for the outdoor performances. (In inclement weather the play moves inside the Großes Festspielhaus where there is no standing room; given Salzburg's mischievous weather, it is not unheard of for the play to begin outside and end up within – causing more than a little confusion.) Occasionally, visitors browsing by the stage entrance are treated to such unexpected sights as the Devil himself – horns, hawk nose and red body – emerging for his role from a chauffeur-driven Mercedes.

The Festival generally runs for five weeks, from the latter part of July to the end of August. Each year shortly before the first performance, there is a palpable excitement in the air as the sounds of voices and instrument in rehearsal fill the air and the spectator benches are erected on the Cathedral Square in readiness for *Jedermann.* On the evening before the official opening ceremony in the Festspielhaus, a grand reception is held at the Residenz in honor of Austria's Federal President. After dining, guests can watch from the windows torchlit folk dancing (Fackeltanz) on the square below. At the end of the dances, the blazing torches are thrown into the fountain plunging the square into complete darkness.

As it was in the 1920s and 1930s, the Salzburg Festival is a veritable fashion show, with cars and taxis lined up in front of the Grosses Festspielhaus discharging their elegantly groomed and designer-dressed passengers, while across the street lines of strollers gape at the fashion parade.*

With so much going on simultaneously during festival time, all possible settings are utilized: large and small concert halls, churches, squares, Summer Riding School, Mozarteum gardens, Land-

---

* Festival tickets are marked in German and English with these words: "Guests are expected to dress in keeping with the festive spirit of the occasion."

estheater, the Residenz. Among the most interesting recent developments has been a "Fest in Hellbrunn." Here, on specially designated days, a mulitfaceted event of some seven hours takes place; the visitor pays one admission price and chooses from among the offerings: ballet, children's theater, chamber music, recitation and opera. Operas are staged in the Steintheater with highly effective results, be the work an old madrigal comedy or a 20th century Benjamin Britten opera. Naturally, Handel's *Water Music* is a fitting accompaniment to Markus Sittikus' water games.

Tickets for the Salzburg Festival are expensive – reportedly the most expensive of all the European festivals. In 1980 the best opera seats went for the equivalent of $ 133 apiece at the box office (and much more on the black market). Yet the range is large, and for $ 26 one could in that same year obtain a balcony seat at the opera. Concert matinees at the Mozarteum are still cheaper, as are the concerts in Mirabell Palace and the Residenz; the latter are not strictly part of the Festival since they run year-round.

Unfortunately, whether or not they attend its performances, Salzburg residents are required to help support it via taxes. The *Land* government has been trying to rectify this inequity by holding a two-week October cultural event with high quality performances and lower prices aimed at attracting Salzburgers. There are also attempts to bring concerts out of town into the nearby villages.

High prices, limited choice of music, exclusive attitude – these invite criticism today of the Salzburg Festival. Yet one is hard pressed to find any other music festival that offers such consistently exciting performances of such deserving works in so remarkable a setting.

CHAPTER EIGHT
MAGICAL MARIONETTES

Puppets performing operas to tape-recorded music? The new-comer to Salzburg may find the idea bizarre, if not downright silly. Yet an evening or two spent at the Salzburg Marionette Theater convinces most skeptics that this unlikely combination makes for a delightful artistic experience.

Founded in 1913 and throughout its long history a family enter-prise, the Salzburg Marionette Theater is one of the proudest tradi-tions of the town. Its success is not only local (the home season generally runs from April through September and includes Christ-mas-New Years and Mozart Week performances) but international. Indeed, the company's Lilliputian wooden figures, each exquisitely carved and clothed, have travelled the world with their human masters and some two and a half tons of stage equipment. Through the years they have played to a total foreign audience of over two million people in thirty nations.

The home theater of the Salzburg marionettes is at Schwarzstrasse 24 next door to the Mozarteum (they are neighbors in spirit as well as geography, since the marionettes specialize in Mozart operas). Seeing them here is a special treat, for all the accoutrements – stage dimensions, acoustics, decor – are right. Incidentally, the Salzburg marionettes should not be considered an amusement for children. Quite the contrary. The company's occasional stagings of fairy tales, usually in September, are sure to enchant the young of any age, but the more characteristic operatic fare is directed to adult musiclovers.

Anton Aicher, founder of the Salzburg Marionette Theater, grew up during the late nineteenth century in a land enamoured of pup-pets. Travelling companies with burlesque folk heroes had long appealed to the Austrian people, and the courts had their own re-fined examples of this genre. Aicher's dream was to create his own marionette theater. A sculptor by profession, he studied the art of marionette making and manipulating in Munich, then devised his own method of constructing the wooden figures so that they were capable of unsual fidelity to human movement. (Marionettes, as distinguished from other puppet forms such as rod, hand or shadow) are string-controlled from overhead. Family and friends joined Anton Aicher in the building of his first stage. On February

121

27, 1913, the Salzburg Marionette Theater made its public debut with *Bastien and Bastienne,* a short opera about a pair of out-of-sorts lovers and a helpful village sorcerer. The work had been written by Mozart at age twelve. Handling the role of the sorcerer was an eleven year-old: Hermann, Anton's younger son.

This opera, which laid the foundation for the troupe's finest productions, was so successful that the Aichers turned their hobby into a profession, renting a large hall where they played for almost half a century. The family, forming the heart of the theater, made, costumed and manipulated the puppets and designed their stage. Skilled musicians as well, the Aichers performed the vocal and instrumental roles. Numerous folk and original plays were added to the repertoire.

World War I, during which the older Aicher son died, slowed down the company's growth and the father's enthusiasm in it. But Hermann was by now deeply interested in puppetry. When, in 1926, he married Elfriede Eschenlohr, whose soprano voice was ideally suited to the delicate puppets, Anton formally gave the theater over to them as a wedding present. Adding experimental works in science fiction to the program, the Aichers began to tour Europe, then the Near East. Financial crises were frequent; it was not, in fact, until the 1960s that the company finally ended up in the black. Still, the troupe persisted, and in 1935 came an invitation to visit Russia. Because that country's theaters were so large, a whole new gallery of oversize puppets had to be constructed. A marionette of ballerina Anna Pavlova was made especially for this trip. The skills of four manipulators working in concert were required in order for her to dance the "Dying Swan" to Saint-Saëns' music. Pavlova took first prize among the puppet theaters at the 1937 World Exhibition in Paris.

After Germany's annexation of Austria, the company was placed under the control of the Nazi authorities and ordered to perform on The Front with an appropriate flavor to their shows. At war's end the audience was a different one – the American occupying forces, who paid in much needed food and other provisions. Damaged during the hostilities, the original theater was eventually condemned and the Aichers recommenced their nomadic existence. By now their two daughters, Gretl and Frick, were skilled puppeteers and an integral part of the company.

In 1952 the Salzburg Marionette Theater brought to the puppet stage for the first time anywhere Mozart's masterful tribute to the human spirit, *Die Zauberflöte (The Magic Flute)*. This remains its crowning achievement; in no season, on no tour, is it absent. For this opera, stage designer Gunther Schneider-Siemssen developed a revolving stage and a bridge above the stage on which the manipulators would stand; this second innovation gave his imaginative sets great depth and thereafter became a standard feature for all productions. At this time the tape recording was first used to replace live performance and gramophone. Beyond the purely technical progress lay something just as important: a realization of the work's spiritual content. It is in the *Magic Flute* that a dimension of beauty very different from the human stage was most effectively realized by the Aichers. Emphasizing the opera's noble innocence, they have captured its perfect fusion of truth and fantasy. Each of the characters (fairy tale prince and princess, birdcatcher, lecherous slave, high priest, queen-of-the-night) seems tailor-made for their stage.

Mozart's allegorical masterpiece *Don Giovanni (Don Juan)* is another staple of the company, as is the lighthearted *Il Seraglio*. With two more stagings, *The Marriage of Figaro* and *Così fan tutte*, the Salzburg Marionette Theater will have produced all of this master's better known operas, a longtime goal. There is no question that puppets and composer are ideally suited to each other – a happy marriage in the town of his birth.

Among the non-Mozart works, Johann Strauss, Jr.'s *Die Fledermaus (The Bat)* is very popular with audiences. In this Viennese goulash of mistaken identities, the marionettes combine grace and style with defiance of gravity. Four can-can ladies in carrot-red hair glide down from the air in a wicked split, a cluster of bat-shaped ballerinas in indecent red *tutus* flies overhead in the drunken jailor's cell, an exuberant prince swings on the high chandelier. A second comic masterpiece in the current repertoire is Rossini's *Barber of Seville,* which brings a host of bumbling, stuttering characters on stage in frenzied action that would taunt a less gifted company into a mass of tangled strings. Newly staged in 1979 was a longtime favorite, Tchaikowsky's ballet *The Nutcracker.*

The marionettes have been playing in their specially designed theater at Schwarzstrasse 24 since 1971. In the lobby are display cases of puppets from the company's history. The auditorium, seating 360, is aglow with crystal. On its walls are angels, depicted in every imaginable celestial pursuit: wafting on clouds, strumming mandolins, blowing trumpets. There are two curtains; the first, of antique red, parts to reveal a second, smaller one which, in turn, opens onto the miniature stage. Audiences tend to be conscious at first of the motionless puppet faces, the overhead strings, the sound of doll-like feet treading the boards; but reality is soon replaced by the magic of theater which makes the impossible possible and turns wood into flesh-and-blood.

Backstage, from the other side of the curtain, things are quite different. Twinkling stars aren't stars at all; they are lightbulbs sewn on veils. The searing flames of hell wouldn't singe a goose; they are mere lighting effects. But that lost magic is more than compensated for by the troupe of people who run, jump and crawl around transforming balconies into pharmacies and ballrooms into jail cells, who with practised gestures lift their puppets from the wings and send those characters on stage to weep or flirt or curtsey or duel. Sometimes there are as many as ten wooden figures in frenetic activity at one corner of the stage while the puppeteers crowd in ceaseless motion above them. Weaving in and out amongst each other, one's head momentarily under another's arm, the artists bend and stretch and balance on one leg, holding onto an overhead bar for support. With their hands and arms they create a language as intricate as the sign language of the deaf. Occasionally they speak to each other in a terse manner, issuing directives so as to avoid entanglement. When occasionally a string snaps, it is replaced with a new one immediately after the character has made his exit, and if a prop is overturned or a puppet caught, a long pronged instrument rights matters from afar. Rarely is the mishap serious enough to cause the curtain to be lowered.

Such strenuous work demands appropriate attire. Standard dress for the puppeteers is slacks, tops and sandals, which allow them freedom to bend with ease; aprons help in sliding motions across the bridge. But even with ideal clothes, equipment and stage, expertise does not come easily in this art. The most critical task faced by the apprentice puppeteer is to reach the degree of technical facility where he or she is free to concentrate on the desired emotion. Training is rigorous and must be started at a young age if neck and back muscles are to bear the strain. Finger, hand and arm exercises develop nimbleness and strength, and years of practice enable the artist to coordinate the separate gestures into flowing, lifelike movement. It is not often that one finds people who will work that long and hard or who are willing to turn from manipulator to stagehand, content to remain behind the scenes while the wooden figures take the stage and praise. The present company, consisting of the Aichers and a group of longtime and treasured associates, numbers under twenty.

Is it worth all the effort, the sacrifices? For some, no; for the dedicated no other life is possible. Says Gretl Aicher, a gracious and vibrant woman whose hands create some of the company's most glorious creations: "If you play puppets all your life, you become one yourself." Thus do the masters become slaves to their own creations.

Such an attitude is integral to the long success of the Salzburg company. It explains comments like this one, also made by Gretl Aicher: "The puppets like to sing Rossini." For her and her colleagues, each marionette has a life of its own, and it is their responsibility to reveal that life through their hands. So at one are the manipulators with their marionettes that sometimes one does not know whether they are referring to puppet or person: "The ostrich is sick today and cannot perform." Even producers hired to create new works are confused; the humans are not visible on stage, so whom do they address with directions? The puppets, of course.

And what of age? The human cast of the Salzburg Marionette Theater maintains a spirit of remarkable youthfulness, due both to the life-giving nature of their art and to its unique quality of agelessness: from backstage the young puppeteer can portray an old part or the old a young one. Among the most striking examples of this versatility in recent years was septuagenarian Hermann Aicher's rendering of the young and ardent Prince Tamino in *Magic Flute*. This kind of dramatic role with its depiction of moods ranging from the pensive to the rapturous or tormented is much more difficult on the marionette stage than is the playing of exaggerated comic roles where acrobatics are second nature.

On June 10, 1977, a gala seventy-fifth birthday party was held in the theater for Hermann Aicher. The president of Austria attended, as did the city's leading citizens. Only weeks later the Aicher family, returning one evening to their house at Mattsee, a small lakeside town just north of Salzburg, found their beloved master lying peacefully upon a field of clover, his life spent. In deference to his love of the theater, not one performance was cancelled. The show, said Gretl Aicher, who upon her father's death assumed leadership of the company, must go on. Hermann Aicher's puppets – those wooden creatures of eternal youth – would continue to dance and sing while backstage, unseen, the humans grieved.

CHAPTER NINE
"SILENT NIGHT" SEASON

The year was 1818, the day December 24, the place just outside Salzburg in the village of Oberndorf. On this Christmas Eve thoughts of peace were especially precious, for long years of Napoleonic battle were finally over.

A young man named Joseph Mohr was assistant pastor at the newly relocated Church of St. Nicholas. Born in Salzburg to an impoverished mother (a knitter by trade) and a soldier who had deserted the army, he was a student of voice, violin and philosophy and had been ordained at the Salzburg Seminary. Pious, strong-willed, generous to a fault, Mohr was worried on this holy eve. With the church organ out of order, how could he provide music to lift up the congregation's spirits? Mohr decided to write some verses, six of them, and took them to his friend Franz Xaver Gruber.

Gruber, the son of linen weavers in Upper Austria, was a teacher in a nearby church who had recently taken on the organ duties at St. Nicholas. He was known to be a creative organist and a good musician. Mohr handed Gruber the lyrics he had written and suggested that Gruber put together a melody for two soloists and choir, with guitar accompaniment replacing the organ. Gruber did so that afternoon and showed his work to Mohr in the evening. Mohr liked it. That very night at midnight mass, the carol "Stille Nacht, Heilige Nacht" ("Silent Night, Holy Night") was performed in the Church of St. Nicholas at Oberndorf near Salzburg. Mohr sang the tenor part and played the guitar accompaniment while Gruber sang bass; the choir did the refrains. As for the villagers, they listened – and loved it.

For a long time "Silent Night" remained locked in its place of origin. The first copy disappeared, never to be found, but Gruber wrote several more, seven of which have been located; they vary somewhat, in melody and rhythm.

Then Mohr left the Oberndorf church; for the occasion Gruber wrote a farewell piece of music which, it is said, caused the assistant pastor to cry like a child.

Finally, years later, the organ builder made it to Oberndorf to replace the old organ. While there, he heard the carol. Recognizing its inspired quality, he brought it back to his home in the Tyrol where it was picked up by the glovemaking and singing Strasser family from the Ziller Valley. No sooner had the Strassers performed it in Leipzig than "Silent Night" was published in a collection as one of "Four real Tyrolean Songs for a Soprano Soloist or Four Voices with Optional Piano Forte Accompaniment." From then on, the song traveled around the world gathering admirers in distant corners and being translated in languages as varied as Catalan and Icelandic, Albanian and Welsh. Brought to America by another singing family, it was again billed a "Tyrolean folk song" while in Norway it was known simply as a "Protestant hymn." In Berlin the Royal Court Choir attributed it to composer (Johann) Michael Haydn. Meanwhile, further regrettable changes in text and melody occurred, probably inadvertently. Eventually Gruber wrote a paper on "The Authentic Occasion of Composition." This did not settle matters and years passed, the controversy later passing into the hands of the Mohr and Gruber descendents. A handbook was published correctly attributing the lyrics to Mohr but the melody to the choirmaster at the nearby town of Hallein. There was also talk that Mohr had written both words *and* music; people who had belonged to Mohr's congregation in the town of Wagrain said that he had made this claim himself. A series of articles ensued in the *Salzburg Chronicle* while a student of Mohr, angered, wrote to a Gruber son: "He [Mohr] would feel it even in his grave, as one says ... if the melody were not attributed to Franz Gruber. The humble composers were far removed from the thought of making a name for themselves; in their piety they were quite overjoyed simply to sing a holy cradle hymn for the Child Jesus. They have their reward in heaven. Rest content, your father is the composer of the melody, Silent Night, Holy Night!"

As for the carol, the greater its fame and followers, the more numerous were the critics who insisted on judging it by pretentious standards which completely overlooked both the composers' intentions and the very qualities of simplicity and childlike reverence that made it so cherished. A Gruber grandson, commented, "What springs up from the heart's conviction, what arises from the best, purest intention paves its own way in spite of formal irregularities and uncalled for criticism."

As often happens, later generations were able to rectify the mistakes of the past. The originators of "Silent Night" are now acknowledged to be Joseph Mohr and Franz Gruber. A museum at Hallein some nine miles outside of Salzburg preserves the musical papers of Gruber who was for many years choirmaster and organist there and who is buried in its churchyard. When it was decided to build a memorial for the two men, the architects, discovering there was no available likeness of the pious pastor Gruber, had to dig up his skull, then at Wagrain, for that purpose. It was subsequently reinterred in the Oberndorf Memorial Chapel, which was completed and blessed in 1937. Steingasse 9 in Salzburg, where he had lived as a child, is marked with a plaque.

The original chapel, whose walls rung in 1818 with the first performance of "Silent Night" is no more; constant flooding of the Salzach resulted in its demise. But every Christmas Eve droves of people come to the village of Oberndorf anyway to attend midnight mass in the memorial chapel and to hear "Stille Nacht, Heilige Nacht" sung by the village choir.*

Austria has a strong heritage of religious tradition spanning the entire year, but no holiday is more laden with intriguing customs than is the Christmas season. Most of these derive from Christian sources, while a few, whose origins lie in ancient pagan rites, later acquired an overlay of Christian reference. Kept alive largely through the efforts of the heritage-conscious Catholic peasants, these rites, beliefs and celebrations, many of which differ from one locale to another, are maintained in the rural areas around Salzburg much as they have been for centuries.

Of major importance to the Austrian holiday is the reproduction in a variety of forms of the search by The Holy Family for shelter, prior to the birth of Jesus. It is customary for groups of villagers, dressed as Mary, Joseph and attendant shepherds, to walk or ride on horseback through the snowy streets, singing carols and ringing bells. Knocking at each door, they are received within and given donations for local charities as well as a bit of food and a glass of *Schnaps*. Similarly, one might encounter a group of caroling, alms-seeking choir boys or men dressed as the Three Wise Men and holding a long pole atop which is a candle-lit star.

Several customs are strongly linked with prophecy. On December 4, for instance, which is St. Barbara's Day, a young unmarried woman places a cherry twig in water; if it blooms by Christmas Eve she will marry the following year. On St. Thomas Day (December 21) each single girl in the Salzburg village of Flachgau must say a

---

* See the bibliography for information on the beautiful book *150 Years Silent Night Holy Night* which deals in depth with this carol.

The Salzburg Marionette Theatre: masterful displays of the fine art of puppetry.

The »Szene der Jugend«, a festival for young people offering many young artists a first chance to perform and prove themselves before an audience and to launch their career.

The Trapp Family Singers as they travelled the world: in the centre Baroness Maria von Trapp. The priest Franz Wasner composed for and conducted the choir; for many years he directed the Santa Maria del Anima Institute in Rome (below with Pope John Paul II).

There is a daily market . . .

crowds in the famous Getreidegasse.

The worldly power of the Prince Archbishops did not last, their sacred power did. For almost the last 1000 years archbishops of Salzburg have had the right to wear the purple robes even though they are not cardinals. Pictured below is the present Archbishop of Salzburg Dr. Karl Berg.

In Oberndorf (Salzburg Province) the Christmas carol »Silent Night, Holy Night« was heard for the first time.

Traditional dance of the »Perchten« during a performance of the Salzburg Advent Singing.

The original score of »Silent Night« by Franz Xaver Gruber (Museum Carolino Augusteum).

Professor Leopold Kohr (left, right Governor Dr. Haslauer) who all his life has propagated a theory of smallness, now back in the country of his birth which has now discovered him and hailed him as a »prophet«.

Oberndorf is the birthplace of the distinguished political philosopher Leopold Kohr who developed the theory that »size governs« and extolled the virtues of smallness long before E. F. Schumacher produced his popular little book »Small is beautiful«.

Born in 1909, the son of a country doctor, Leopold Kohr graduated and attained his doctorate in law from the University of Innsbruck and then went on to take a second doctorate in political science at the University of Vienna. He also spent terms at the London School of Economics and the Faculté de Droit in Paris. After a period in Spain as correspondent on the civil war for French and Swiss newspapers he emigrated to North America where, after an unusual start, — six weeks hard manual work in a gold mine — his academic career began. He was appointed to the economics faculty of Rutgers University and was later invited to the University of Puerto Rico where he lectured for twenty years. In 1957 one of his major works »The Breakdown of Nations« was published in which Kohr put forward the thesis that bigness is the source of all social misery and that gargantuan growth has caused wars, depressed living standards and blocked social progress. The ideas proposed in this book concerning small states and independent nations were especially warmly received in Wales, struggling for autonomy from Britain and Wales was the next station in Leopold Kohr's career. He lectured at the University College of Wales and became intensively associated with the Welsh nationalist movement, at that time under the leadership of the pacifist Gwynfor Evans.

Now retired from an active academic life, Kohr has returned to Salzburg where in 1981 he was awarded the Ring of the Province of Salzburg by the Landeshauptmann (Provincial Governor) of Salzburg. »The city of Salzburg«, says Leopold Kohr, »represents the perfection of human endeavour . . . the creativity of smallness.«

The Oberndorf Salt Marine Guard

One of the most beautiful views to be had of Salzburg is from the »Café Winkler« restaurant on the Mönchsberg. Typical Salzburg dishes such as the famous »Salzburger Nockerl« are offered on the menu here. Next to the restaurant is a casino for roulette, baccara and black jack.

outside the Residence. After the concert is over, the Glockenspiel is likely to turn out a characteristically off-key rendition of "O Sanctissima." It's a welcome break in the day's shopping. Then, on December 24, at around 5 p.m. carols are played by trumpets from the rocks above St. Peter's; with candles lit by the graves and in the windows of the catacombs, the tableau is memorable.

Reasonably priced chamber music afternoons and evenings in Mirabell palace's Marble Room, bedecked in greenery and flowers, are especially attractive at Christmas. Rather higher in price are the customary holiday appearances of the Salzburg Marionette Theater, the high point being a New Year's Eve performance of that intoxicating operetta *Die Fledermaus,* with champagne available during the intermission.

More difficult to obtain tickets for and more expensive yet are two prestigious Salzburg events. One, in the folk tradition, is the Advent Singing *(Adventsingen)*. Begun in 1945 by Tobi Reiser (founder of the Heimatwerk, Salzburg's mecca of folk art) along with poet Karl Heinrich Waggerl, it was originally a modest, homespun effort at holiday music-making, which met in a small room of the Mozarteum. So popular did it become that before long the group had to move to the Archbishop's Residence, then to the Grosses Festspielhaus where as many as twelve sold-out performances are now presented to a total audience annually of 25,000. The intimacy is surely gone but the group tries to maintain the old folk spirit. Along with carols are poetry recitations, dances, instrumental solos and choral selections by many local groups. A quintet composed of guitar, dulcimer (an ancient instrument), harp, zither and contrabass plays music from such areas as the Pongau and other districts in the Province of Salzburg. At the heart of Advent Singing, actually a medieval form, is once again the search of Mary and Joseph for shelter; this is carried out in two-part antiphony, one choir answering another. Admittedly, it is the German-speaking people in the audience who most appreciate this long and varied fare with its dependence on local dialects and in-humor.

The single most important event of a classical nature during the holiday season also takes place in the Large Festival House, but only on one evening. This is the presentation of a great religious work, most often Bach's *Christmas Oratorio,* by such outstanding groups as the Munich Bach Choir and Orchestra. In the great hall the audience dresses in its finest: the women in gowns or long *Dirndl* dresses, men in dinner jackets or the traditional *Trachten* suits. Because the work to be performed is generally of substantial length, it has been customary to schedule one lengthy intermission during which attendees could take off for a festive meal at a nearby restaurant. Recently, however, a new practice was initiated whereby only one half of the composition was given in an evening, the other half being scheduled the following year. As a result the audience felt both rather taken price-wise and left hanging music-wise. Another very popular series is known as the "Gang durch den Advent" with four concerts of seasonal prose and music given on the four Saturdays in Advent in the University Hall.

By the time Salzburg residents get to New Year's Eve they are usually exhausted and several pounds heavier, but this does not stop them from partaking of their time-honored dinner of *Krenfleisch* (pig's head, belly, feet and shoulder, flavored with horseradish); a feast of pork is supposed to bring luck for the coming year. At midnight fireworks are set off on the Untersberg; on a clear night people stand below watching the brilliant streaks of color flash across the sky. Those too cold to venture out stay home with family or friends drinking wine or champagne and indulging in a popular entertainment called *Bleigiessen:* they put balls of lead in ladles and melt them over a candle or in the fireplace, then pour the melted lead into a pan or bowl of cold water. The resultant shapes are interpreted to reveal the futures of the participants.

On a snowy New Year's Day, if one is not glued to the TV set with the Vienna Philharmonic in its annual medley of waltzes, one might engage in some cross-country skiing near Hellbrunn Castle, or, if Lake Leopoldskron has obligingly frozen over, lots of people walk over for skating. It's a colorful scene: mittened hands and stocking-capped heads, toddlers falling and adults showing off, dogs sliding about making a nuisance of themselves among the curling games and ice hockey pucks. Huddled at the edge of the slippery glaze begging for handouts are the lake's noisy ducks, its elegant, if ill-tempered, swans. Gradually the day passes, the afternoon darkening into a rosy sunset, and too soon it is time to go home. The holidays are almost over.

But not quite. On January 6 (Epiphany) the combined Celtic-Christian heritage makes its presence known in Salzburg. On this Twelfth Night of Christmas a long procession of young men known as Bell Runners *(Glöcklerlaufen)* winds in and out the snowy squares of town in figure 8 formation. They dress in white with

huge cowbells tied to their waists and wear heavy, handmade head-
dresses of wood and paper which are lit from within. The latter are
now in the shapes of Christian symbols; this was a 19th century
change, initiated after strong Church disapproval of the heathen
custom. The exact origin of Bell Running is not clear; probably the
ceremony was intended to bring luck to the fields. Today, seeing the
eerily beautiful figures in their ritualized formation, one can imagine a similar scene in the Salzburg – the Juvavum – of two thousand
years ago.

CHAPTER TEN
WHERE JULIE ANDREWS DANCED

What Mozart and the summer festival did not do for Salzburg in terms of fame and money, "The Sound of Music" did.

The continued popularity – indeed, the mystique – of this 1965 Twentieth Century Fox movie, photographed in and around Salzburg, is something of a puzzle to the natives, who never particularly took to it. (Dubbed rather amateurishly in German and retitled "My Dreams, My Songs", it closed halfway through the initial run). But in the U.S the film won five Oscars and beat even "Gone with the Wind" in box office attendance. Even today moviegoers from all over the world flock into Salzburg with their tripods, wide-angle lenses and memories of Maria, alias Julie Andrews and seven motherless children.

The story of the singing Trapp family was a natural for Hollywood. As the real Maria, later Baroness von Trapp, tells it in one of her several books, she was born in a train en route to the Tyrol, lost both her mother and father by the time she was nine, and was given over to an uncle who sent her to a socialist school, scorned her religious fervor, beat her and ended up himself in a asylum for the insane. Then she went on to a new life. Determined to renounce her freedom as a demonstration of love of God, she ran off from a hiking group and sought the cloistered life, asking as soon as she got to Salzburg, "Which is the strictest convent in town?" She was directed to the ancient abbey of Nonnberg.

It was here that Hollywood picked up the story. Orphan Maria, a not too successful novice at Nonnberg (she was always off climbing hills) was sent to care for the children of the widowed Baron Georg von Trapp, who had been commander of an Austrian submarine during World War I. First the children and then middle-aged Trapp fell for Dirndl-clad, guitar-strumming Maria, and eventually he chose to marry her instead of an older woman of his own social class. The family sang its way through happy times together, gradually turning what had been a hobby into a profession. Then, encountering the spectre of Hitler, the Trapps decided to risk all and give up home and homeland rather than succumb to his evil. In 1938 they emigrated to the U.S with their musical advisor and friend, Father Wasner, an Austrian priest.

This is substantially the time period covered in the film. Had Hollywood chosen, it could have continued the story, for the Trapp adventures did not end with their departure from Austria. Along with some twenty years of concertizing and missionary work around the world, they took up another business in their adopted country: hotel management. Buying up 600 acres of land in Vermont's choice ski country, at Stowe, they turned a farmhouse into a Salzburg-style chalet and began to have guests on an increasingly large scale. At the chalet they took to celebrating an annual Trapp Family Christmas, organized a Trapp Family Camp, set up a Trapp Family Gift Shop which featured Trapp Family postcards and bottled their own Trapp Family Natural Spring Water from the Green Mountain State. It's quite a story and quite a business. The young novice Maria, who years before had climbed the 144 steps to Nonnberg Convent for the first time, would never have believed it.

The making of the film was big business of another variety. It all began back in 1949 when Maria Augusta Trapp wrote her first book, an autobiography called *The Story of the Trapp Family Singers*. A German company, Gloria Films, developed an interest in the story and sent an agent to discuss this with her. As she confides in a later tome, *Maria*, the agent talked her into selling the film rights upon payment of $ 9,000. Royalties, he evidently told her, could not be paid by a German company to a foreigner – a statement she later determined to be untrue. The producer of the German film and a sequel to it was none other than the Baroness' fellow countryman Wolfgang Reinhardt, one of two sons of Max Reinhardt.

Next on the scene was Broadway. Leland Hayward and Oscar Hammerstein II saw the makings of a musical play, followed by a Hollywood movie; the first would star Mary Martin of "South Pacific" fame. Martin's husband Richard Halliday spent eight fruitless months trying to locate Baroness von Trapp for permission to be depicted on stage as at the time she was in the South Pacific doing missionary work. (The Baron had died in 1947.) Halliday finally caught up with her as her boat docked in San Francisco, after which the several and widely scattered Trapp children also had to be reached for similar clearance. Then it took six months for terms to be agreed upon with the German film company, which technically still owned the movie rights. It seems, according to a *New York Times* article, that Wolfgang Reinhardt insisted on a fraction of a per cent – a sum which has enabled him to live not uncomfortably in Rome since. Maria von Trapp admits to having been treated "nobly" by Broadway: royalties plus a salary to teach Mary Martin the

Ländler, an Austrian folk dance. The two women grew to like each other, Martin presenting the Baroness with a pale green evening dress to wear on opening night.

"The Sound of Music" was a gamble for Broadway, one which paid off handsomely. Though critics were divided – some calling it moving and glorious while others dismissed it as sugary and sentimental – audiences were not. The advance sales exceeded $ 3 million, the show ran for over four years, and the Rogers and Hammerstein tunes echoed from one end of America to the other.

Baroness von Trapp was pleased with Broadway's "Sound of Music" and with its general attitude. She was not so pleased with Hollywood's subsequent treatment of her, claiming that she never was even informed directly of her forthcoming immortalization on celluloid. Learning of this only through "rumors and hearsay," she attempted to contact producer Robert Wise, hoping to clarify certain scenes where the play had not been entirely accurate. For instance, she felt Broadway's portrayal of her husband had been rather harsh. But Wise, she reports, was not about to soften the characterization or to listen to her at all, claiming that he was not concerned about either persons or facts. And, when the movie appeared, says the snubbed Baroness, there was no seat for her at the first official showing, so she had to go on her own.

Hollywood did take many liberties with Maria Trapp's story, just as had Broadway. These are the ways of the entertainment world. It is precisely such inaccuracies, however, that bother natives of Salzburg, many of whom knew the Trapp family personally. They point out particular diversions from fact. Having been raised with the genuine Trapp music, which was of folk and religious origin, they are not responsive to tunes like "Do re mi" and "How do you solve a problem like Maria?" Similarly, they find the geography to be downright confusing: Hollywood, they feel, took the map of Salzburg and environs, cut it into the pieces of a jigsaw puzzle, and put the pieces back but in the wrong place. The Trapps never lived at Leopoldskron Palace where tourists arrive daily looking for leftover stage sets, but at 34 Traunstrasse in the suburban village of Aigen. (The Trapp villa, cream-colored with green shutters, lies almost hidden behind a stone wall which was erected by an S.S. leader who occupied the villa during the war; now it is owned by a religious community.) And the real Maria wasn't married in the church of

Mondsee, many miles distant, but in the same Nonnberg Convent where she was a novice. Not the least of the mislocations took place at the end of the film when the Trapps supposedly were escaping from Nazi-occupied territory to neutral Switzerland; had the family taken the same route as Hollywood's, up the Untersberg mountain, they would have ended up not in neutral Switzerland but in Germany, just a stone's throw from Hitler's "Eagle's Nest"!

But most significant to the negative Austrian attitude is the subject matter of "Sound of Music": World War II – something that they want to forget. That nightmare was real to them in a way it can never be to people on whose ground it was not fought.

The outside world, of course, saw and still sees entirely different things in "The Sound of Music": magnificent snow-covered peaks, lilting tunes, young love (incidentally, enticing Julie Andrews bore little resemblance to solidly built Maria Trapp), and fearless heroism – a perfect combination for escapist entertainment. As a result of its enormous success, there has been a consistently large upsurge of tourism in the Salzburg area. Capitalizing on this are business enterprises and gimmicks of every variety: a phonograph record shop calling itself "Sound of Music", venders selling straw flowers laced with edelweiss after the song of that name, tourist stalls stocked with "Sound of Music" calendars and fold-out postcards. And the local post office has been known to meter its mail with "Salzburg, City of Sound of Music". Most successful of all is the American Express "Sound of Music Tour" which takes busloads of people, some 5,000 annually, to the locales featured in the film; the original soundtrack is piped in.

Salzburg residents tell a number of amusing stories connected with the filming. One of these concerns the particular hill selected for a Julie Andrews nature walk. Lovely it was, but it lacked the necessary shimmering body of water.

Undaunted, Hollywood created a makeshift tinfoil-bottomed lake, paying the local owner well for use of his land. A neighbor, jealous of the deal, punched holes one night in the tin foil, causing the said water to run out. The crew had to send fire engines back up to refill it and took the additional measure of ringing their artificial lake with police.

It's a good subject for gossip and a better one for business. After all, though Salzburg residents may not all be pleased with the *reason* some people come to their lovely town, they are generally quite willing to have them.

As for the visitors, who can blame us for taking refuge in the make-believe world of "Sound of Music" and for wishing that we, too, could follow the Rogers and Hammerstein advice to

"Climb every mountain,
Ford every stream,
Follow every rainbow
Till you find your dream."

CHAPTER ELEVEN
GUSTATORY DIVERSIONS

"*Mahlzeit!*" say Austrians to each other as they sit down to an over-flowing table. ("Enjoy your meal!")

Foreigners often find the frequency – let alone the portions – of these repasts to be rather staggering. For traditionalists, there is, to begin with, the early breakfast *(Frühstück)* of crisp *Semmeln* (rolls, hard on the outside and soft inside) served with jam and butter, and coffee. Next, in mid morning is *Gabel Frühstück* (literally, "fork breakfast") when some meat and a beer will help still the hunger pangs until the next proper meal: lunch or *Mittagessen*. Lunch is not a tea sandwich kind of meal; it includes soup, meat, a starch (noodles, rice or potatoes), salad, bread, dessert and coffee. *Jause*, or afternoon tea, is more accurately an excuse for pastry, several tiers in height. Supper *(Abendessen)*, eaten rather late, can be similar in character to lunch or, for the faint-hearted, a pick-up meal of cold meats. (Admittedly, many Austrians have taken to lighter eating in these diet- and health-conscious times.)

From the former Habsburg Empire Austria inherited a variety of dishes – Slavic, Turkish, Italian, Magyar, German – and adapted them for home consumption, along with her native foods. On the whole, the resultant dishes are hearty and flavorful, if sometimes lacking in subtlety and delicacy. The great contribution of the country to cuisine is its baked desserts, most notably the rich cakes known as *Torten*, and its bread; both are among the best in the world.

Salzburg cooking cannot be clearly differentiated from that of neighboring areas, though in general it is considered to be more robust and rustic than Viennese cooking and lighter than Bavarian. Basically, it is the kind of food that for centuries has appealed to the mountain folk who labored physically in an often harsh winter climate. On the other hand, there have also been more sophisticated influences, such as the brief period of French occupation which added a soupçon of gallic spice to the diet. And then there were the pampered and paunchy archbishops, many of them from Bohemia or Italy, who demanded variety and dash in their diet and often brought their cooks to Salzburg for this purpose.

The royal reputation for good food was never put to more cunning use than by Archbishop Leonhard von Keutschach who, wanting to capture his town councillors, invited them all to dinner, then treated them instead to an icy sleigh ride.

Leonhard's successors ate well, too, and so (occasionally) did the townspeople. When royalty visited Salzburg there was feasting not only in the archbishop's own residence but in town for all citizens. Kitchens were set up in the squares and long banquet tables groaned with food, while fountains spouted wine from the Tyrol and Lower Austria. The archbishops paid careful attention to the menus, specifying such exacting requirements as turkey gizzards stuffed with peppercorns and wrapped in bay leaves.

These repasts must have been quite delicious, for Hans Sachs, the 16th century German cobbler and master singer, saw fit in a song about Salzburg to rhapsodize over the local cheese, beer, fish and fowl, and a certain Bavarian duke sent his personal cook here to improve his kitchen technique; he was especially directed to learn how to make good noodles. The municipal tavern also had quite a following by this time, for reason of its fish as well as its libation.

We know a good deal today about Salzburg foods and meals of the past largely because the town seemed to have been as interested in recording what it ate as in the actual eating. Weddings of leading residents were described with each course and food specified (artichokes and Westphalian hams, venison and trout – in all, 25 or 30 dishes would be consumed). In 1719, the year Mozart's father was born, the *New Salzburg Cookbook* by one Conrad Hagger was published, a compendium of cookery some five inches thick, over six pounds heavy and with more than 2500 dishes.

Such concern with food naturally had a long-term effect on the citizenry as a whole, and Salzburg families today devote a lot of thought (and money) to good eating. Supermarkets are no different here than elsewhere in the developed world, but people depend more on the little specialty shops, buying their bread here, cheese there, smoked meat at yet another place. Neighborhoods and even streets are known for particular items – Linzergasse, for instance, has gingerbread bakers. Very popular are the colorful outdoor markets located on the University Square near the Collegiate Church and across the river by St. Andrew's Church. (The first is the so-called Green Market and is open every day except Thursday; it's best on Saturday mornings. The other is open Thursday mornings only.) Full of fresh, tempting farm produce, they are direct descendants of the cattle, fish and food markets of centuries past.

142

Eating the food is as pleasant as buying it in this setting. Rarely does a *Wurst* (sausage) taste so good as it does at one of these outdoor stands, where it is served piping hot on a fresh roll with mild or hot mustard. While chewing, one is kept busy examining various vegetables like radishes piled in high pyramids or small yellow mushrooms in baskets, poultry, berries, sweet-smelling country bread, and a variety of flowers with which to decorate the table. Manning the stalls are farm families from around Salzburg who are obliged to obtain a yearly license in order to run their businesses.

Salzburg is a town of restaurants. Among the best known are those associated with hotels; they tend to be expensive. The Goldener Hirsch ("Golden Stag"), housed in a very old inn whose guest rooms are furnished with fine rustic pieces, is so popular at festival time that dinner reservations often have to be made months in advance. Favored members of the audience come here during intermission for a course or two, return to the Grosses Festspielhaus, and finish up after the final curtain with a rich dessert. Another leading hotel is the Österreichischer Hof (known familiarly as the Ö.H.) whose Grill and Cellar are popular for after-performance eating.

The most elaborate meal of the year in these and other leading restaurants is the annual *Heringschmaus* feast; this is the traditional Ash Wednesday supper (sometimes also eaten on Shrove Tuesday) featuring cold platters, sour herring being predominant. In the old days it was, surprisingly, the railway station restaurant that had the best *Heringschmaus* of all.

Often more reasonably priced are the charming native restaurants and *Gasthäuser* (guest houses), the latter also offering overnight accommodation. The decor is likely to be simple and cheerful, with highly polished old wooden floors and beamed ceilings. In these establishments large portions of hearty food emerge from the kitchen – liver dumpling soup, several varieties of veal *(Schnitzel)*, trout, venison, shish kebab (called *Zigeunerspiess,* or "gypsy food"), mixed grill platters ringed with fresh vegetables. For big eaters the *Bauernschmaus,* or "peasant's feast," combines ham, pork and sausage with dumplings and sauerkraut. These dishes are washed down with beer or the house wine, served in open flasks. Desserts are also on the heavy side: a special dish made with eggs, currants, raisins, and sugar known as *Kaiserschmarrn,* thick, sweet pancakes filled with chocolate or jam *(Palatschinken),* or various kinds of sweet dumplings (yeast, apricot and plum) called *Knödl.*

Less filling but more potent are the fruits steeped in rum or the ice cream covered with hot berries and liqueur.

One need not remain in the center of town for dining. Delightful restaurants are located in the outskirts, across the border in Germany and in the lake/mountain region, Salzkammergut. Some are located atop gentle mountain peaks and look down on verdant fields populated by lazy, well fed cows – the gentle tinkle of their bells filling the air. In summer, the locals spend whole afternoons at these hideaways. Seated out on the terrace in their mountain climbing gear and jaunty Tyrolean hats, they munch away at *Leberkäse* (a processed meat specialty), swill a mug of beer or apple juice, and doze in the sun. Conversely, in winter, guests sit inside in cozy comfort with steaming bowls of goulash soup, looking out of the big windows over snowy peaks. In truth, dining in this part of the world is as notable for its scenery as for its food.*

Going from a mountain top down to the cellar is not as depressing as it may sound, especially if it is for wine or beer. No one knows just when the town turned to beer, but a chronicle of the 12th century describes the activities of brewers in Salzburg at the time. Three centuries later that unappealing archbishop, Leonhard, played yet another dirty trick: he tried to monopolize the breweries, buying two of them and decreeing that the innkeepers and tavern owners sell only his beer. But residents of Salzburg didn't like the royal mix and began to call him jestingly Liendlwirt ("Leonhard, the Tavern Owner"). Other breweries were founded which better suited their tastes, including Stiegl-Bräu which remains today a major local industry.

Many archbishops besides Leonhard took an active interest in this subject. One of them, Count Lichtenstein, who came from Bohemia (the land of superior beer), tried to introduce his native brewing methods, but his employees didn't appreciate this and went on strike. Lichtenstein put them in jail and drafted some in the army as punishment.

Salzburgers to this day are very choosy about their beer – be it for light or dark, native or imported, this brew or that – but they all seem to agree that it tastes best in the Bavarian atmosphere of a beer hall. Here they can, if they wish, bring their own food to accom-

---

* If, after a while, you've had enough meals of noodles and sauerkraut, you might try a change of nationality. Salzburg has everything from Mexican to Chinese food; its Yugoslav cuisine is especially fine at the Weisses Kreuz Restaurant.

pany the main item. Sunday afternoon live music and outdoor gardens for summer imbibing are added attractions. The vast Stieglkeller is one favorite spot, and the Sternbräu, located in a very old part of town, was frequented by eminent beer drinkers of the past, including W.A. Mozart. Many of the beer halls were once breweries as well; the Augustinerbräu in Mülln continues this dual role today.

Unlike beer, wine is not an important industry in Salzburg. At one time vineyards were active here, but the resultant beverage was of a poor quality, so that early on most wines were imported. The wine cellar of St. Peter's Monastery has a special and interesting history. In the year 1044 the Margrave Leopold gave to the monastery as a gift the Dornbach vineyard near Vienna. The monks began then to make their own fine wines, transporting these to Salzburg where they utilized the cool caves in the Mönchsberg as a natural cellar. By the mid 17th century they were selling the wine and, later, food as well. Today Peterskeller (Peter's Cellar) is one of Salzburg's best known eating places, cozy and warm in winter and with summer dining outside directly under the mountain. Like most of the cellars, Peter's looks happiest when it is full of people and noise – and that is most of the time.*

Coffee houses, which once were a seemingly permanent feature of such cities as Paris, are now a rarity; the rapid pace of life on the continent is making them obsolete. But in Salzburg, as in Vienna, these remain a charming holdover from earlier, more peaceful times, a place where you can sit for much longer than it takes for you to finish your cup.

Coffee houses stretch from one end of Salzburg to the other. To understand their popularity, one need only consider the hours of one old-timer: the Café Bazar, located near the Mozarteum. The Bazar (which Bauer calls "an oriental excrescence from the turn of the century") is open from 7:30 a.m. to 11 p.m. daily except Sundays and holidays when it opens a half-hour later. Another is Tomaselli, a direct successor to the first coffee house in town begun in 1703 by a Frenchman. The present Tomaselli is on Alter Markt (the "Old Market-Place"), at the heart of the festival district. Sitting up on the flower-festooned terrace one can see the bustle of the city below and, on Sundays during the Festival, hear the calls of *Everyman* echoing through town.

* As new as Peterskeller is old is the Rainbergkeller, which was fashioned from the rock of that ancient mountain.

How the cafés remain in business with their restricted menus (most serve only desserts and beverages) and their sedentary clientele is something of a mystery. Admittedly, the price of that cup of coffee is steep, but you are paying both for the ambience and for the luxury of choosing from so many varieties. To name a few, coffee with hot milk is preferred at breakfast, *Mokka* (very strong, black, with sugar) for after a substantial meal, and *mit Schlag* (with heavy whipped cream floating seductively on top) for mid afternoon. Those whose waistlines do not concern them go all the way with *Doppelschlag* (a double order of whipped cream) or, in summer, *Eiskaffee* (coffee laced both with *Schlag* and ice cream).

One sees a special side of Salzburg in its coffee houses. In this pleasant atmosphere deals are consummated, letters written, phone calls received, newspapers read (they are presented to regular customers on a wire rack), assignations planned, performances reviewed, gossip rendered and philosophies aired.

Given that Austria's great contribution to the world of cuisine is its desserts, it is only natural that there are eating places known as *Konditoreien,* or confectioners' shops, which specialize in all those rich pastries. The temptations are featured in display windows: apple or plum *Strudel*, hazelnut cake, *Sachertorte* (that famous Viennese chocolate cake coated with apricot jam and iced with more chocolate) and *Linzertorte* (the Linz version, flavored with almonds and red currant marmalade). Sometimes the line between the coffee shops and the *Konditoreien* is a fine one, but on the whole the former maintain a more placid air.

One cannot leave the subject of Salzburg cuisine without mention of its most famous dessert, the *Salzburger Nockerl.*

Literally, the dish means "Salzburg dumpling," but actually it is quite different: a sweet, airy egg concoction baked briefly in a hot oven; it should be light and creamy within but firmly shaped so that it does not collapse on its way to the table. When prepared by the wizard chef, the *Salzburger Nockerl* is a visual as well as gustatory delight: it emerges on a tray in mounds – veritable Alpine peaks, golden brown, and topped with a sprinkling of powdered sugar. Rumor has it that this dish was created for Napoleon, but its actual origin is unknown. It is said in Salzburg that there are as many recipes for this dessert as there are people, and each restaurant of note has its own version which, in the manner of the *Mozart Kugel,* is claimed to be the *echte* or "real" one.

ser's philosophy in the person of his son, also Tobi, who has been manager since the elder Reiser's death.

Walking into this emporium (the word "store" does not seem to do it justice), one is confronted with myriad examples of peasant craft. Imaginatively displayed, they fill room after room: carved chests, straw wickerwork, printed linen, woven tablecloths, fringed shawls, painted Christmas tree decorations, green and white Gmundner ceramic ware, bouquets of dried flowers, pewter urns, paintings on glass, wax wall hangings, *Schnaps* bottles and the traditional wine dispensers called *Weinheber* – where to start buying and *how* to stop?

Tobi Reiser, Senior, had another great interest and that was music. Here his desire was much the same: to retain old instruments and pieces, modifying them for modern times. It was Reiser who with others founded the now famous annual Christmas Advent Singing and who brought back into popularity an ancient stringed instrument, the *Hackbrett*, making it smaller and more versatile; thanks to him there are currently about a thousand *Hackbrett* players in Austria and Bavaria. Reiser began his own instrumental ensemble which performed light folk music, typical of Salzburg. The young Tobi Reiser has carried on this tradition, too, playing guitar in a nine person ensemble.

The *Heimatwerk*, in collaboration with the public office *Heimatpflege* (literally, "cultivation of the homeland"), must also be given credit for the systematic revival of Salzburg's traditional attire, the *Trachten*, which many other cities in Austria, including Vienna, have discarded except for ceremonial occasions. It was an eminently successful effort, and the enthusiasm of citizens for their native dress is a matter of great local pride. This is not to say that the modish and the chic in fashion do not exist here – they do, or, rather, they co-exist naturally with the *Trachten*, often in the same person's wardrobe.

Residents of Salzburg have long been interested in clothes and the materials from which they are made. Historians have traced certain of the fabrics used in today's garments back to Roman and even Celtic times: the rough sheep's wool known as *Loden*, for instance, popular today as a sturdy, rain- and snow-resistant material for overcoats and capes (the traditional color is olive green) and the leather which is standard for men's attire.

As wealth and sophistication came to Salzburg during the centuries of archbishops' rule, the peasant folk began to imitate courtly

151

attire, using their own hand-woven materials. Many farmers disapproved of this practice, complaining that their workers, male and female, were spending too much on dress and consequently asking for exorbitant wages. Archbishop Jakob Graf von Dietrichstein, who took office in 1747, was also displeased. In an attempt to restore the archbishopric's faltering finances and the peasants' modesty of manner, he produced a decree against luxuriousness in dress which is quoted in Kant's book: "When a person is found to dress in an unbecoming and improper way, the clothes shall be cut into pieces and the person shall be put to jail for eight days with nothing to eat but dry bread and water, provided that he (or she) does not buy himself (or herself) out by paying a fine ..."

In the end it was the standard peasant dress rather than the impractical courtly attire that stood the test of time and constitutes the current manner of Salzburg folk dress. The eighteenth century was a golden age for native costume, with almost every village in Land Salzburg possessing its own distinct patterns and color combinations (an expert can easily distinguish a Pongau *Tracht* from a Pinzgau one or from a Flachgau one). It was in the Pongau region that, immediately prior to World War I, the movement for a renaissance of 18th century garb began, spreading through the Alpine lands. Today many local clubs and agricultural schools work together with the *Heimatpflege* and Reiser's *Heimatwerk*, putting on a yearly show that features traditional attire in modern adaptations. Lighter-weight materials and occasional new color combinations are approved, but the whims and fads of fashion are not accepted, including arbitrarily raised or lowered skirts; nor are synthetic fabrics allowed. Believing that natives who wear the *Trachten* should have a special relationship with them, the *Heimatwerk* stocks no ready-made items – only the materials; a customer may choose however, to have an outfit custom-made here. For ready-made garments there are many *Trachten* shops in Salzburg, the best known being Lanz on Schwarzstrasse, which has been in existence for half a century and has a branch in California.

The standard outfit for women is the three-piece *Dirndlkleid* ("girl's dress"); over the years it has become known simply as the *Dirndl*. The Salzburg version is composed of a figured, hand-printed cotton skirt to which is attached a sleeveless bodice of peasant linen with a deep round or square neckline. A special white blouse (often with eyelit trim) is worn under the bodice, and a half apron tied at the waist has a pattern different from but complementary to the skirt. Only certain color and fabric combinations are proper, and to be deemed a good fit the waist and bodice must be so tight as to be downright uncomfortable. Traditional accessories include hand-knitted white knee socks, fringed scarf, buckled shoes and a several stranded choker necklace. The *Dirndl* is considered appropriate for all ages, all occasions. A long version for evening wear utilizes such fabrics as rich silk brocade for the skirt matched with shimmering silk aprons.

The male counterpart is the *Trachten* suit of grey wool with green lapels or small standing collar; like the *Dirndl* it is worn for a variety of occasions, formal or informal. For hiking, the native male generally wears his *Lederhosen*, leather pants, grey or black in color and made of deer-, calf- or horseskin. They come in knickerbocker (three-quarter) length or short for summer.* Probably the most practical trousers in existence, *Lederhosen* often outlive their owners. Only when the seat of the pants are brilliantly shiny from wear are they considered top quality. Common accessories are long wool socks of olive green, red or grey, and a black or green felt hat which sports a huge *Gamsbart* (chamois hair) or trophies.

Tradition, custom, heritage: these, then, are important concepts in Salzburg. But what of the new, the experimental, the modern? These, in contrast, are often jarring to the city's image of itself, and the juggling of the two extremes is perhaps the greatest dilemma the city faces today. Yet the old and the new need not be contradictory or disharmonious any more than the traditionalist must be old and the innovator young.

Music is, of course, the field upon which Salzburg's fame chiefly rests. The summer festival, given inspiration by the works of Mozart, generally has a very conservative program.

Admittedly, the summer festival has taken some suggestive moves in the direction of modernity, including performances of contemporary operas and even a new overture to replace the standard Mozart work at the formal beginning of the 1977 season. But its audiences are not very receptive to such fare, and the people who *would* be receptive can't afford to go. Obviously, the most effective vehicle for modern music are special organizations created with youth and the new in mind.

---

* Alas, the short ones are seen less these days, having lost center stage to that most un-Austrian item of attire: blue jeans.

In that regard, the "Szene der Jugend" ("Youth Scene") is particularly important. Begun in 1971 as an means of interesting Salzburg's younger residents in culture they could both afford and relate to, it was spearheaded by Alfred Winter, journalist Gottfried Kraus, composer César Bresgen, artists and students who called themselves Club 2000 in clear reference to the upcoming century. From a free art show along the banks of the River Salzach, it has emerged as one of the most innovative European festivals of music (Bach to Rock and back to Renaissance) with many additional art forms: film, painting, photography, theater, puppetry, literature readings and pottery, among these. Utilizing unknown performers along with established ones (pianist Friedrich Gulda is a regular here and violinist Gidon Kremer has declared his affinity to the ambiance of the "Szene"), the "Szene" caters for casually dressed audiences of all ages who pay a minimal price (generally from 30 to 50 AS) to attend its imaginative offerings.

The "Szene der Jugend" has on occasion been referred to as Salzburg's "counter-festival," and, in some respects it does run counter to the main festival's traditions and present philosophy. Furthermore, certain of its presentations have been intended precisely to jar Salzburg's sensiblities. There was, for instance, "Col," a group of Swiss journalists, painters, psychologists, teachers and film people who went from square to square one summer under the auspices of the "Szene der Jugend", inviting the public to take part in an experiment of open communication. "What do you really think of von Karajan?" they would ask, and in drawings and posters the audience expressed its honest reactions to the almost legendary *maestro* whose silver-grey Rolls Royce with the Swiss license plates is the town's best known vehicle. Then there was *Jede Frau (Every Woman)*, a play loosely concerned with the emancipation of women but more basically a not very subtle takeoff of everything that Salzburg reveres from *Everyman* to Mozart.

Such irreverence has a purpose beyond merely rejecting the accepted and acceptable. Rather, "Szene der Jugend" seeks to involve its audiences creatively, to free them from the bonds of tradition and broaden their artistic experience. Many people in Salzburg have come to feel a part of the "Szene" in a way they no longer can with the big festival which has simply become too expensive and snobbish, the tickets impossible to obtain, the expected dress excessively formal. In an important sense, then, the "Youth Scene" has taken

154

Peternell, Pert, editor. *Salzburg Chronik.* Salzburg, 1971.

Rech, Geza. *Visiting Mozart.* Salzburg, n. d.

Rickett, Richard. *A Brief Summary of Austrian History.* Vienna, 1975.

Rinnerthaler, Reinhard M. *Photo-Guide to Salzburg.* Salzburg, 1974.

Saylor, Oliver M., editor. *Max Reinhardt and his Theater.* London, 1968.

Schlegel, Richard. *Official Guide to the Castle of Hohensalzburg.* Salzburg, 1955.

Schmaus, Alois and Kriss-Rettenbeck, Lenz, editors. *150 Years Silent Night History and Circulation of a Carol.* Innsbruck, 1968.

Schmiedbauer, Alois. *Salzburg: Gestalt und Antlitz.* Salzburg, 1973.

Schonberg, Harold C. *The Lives of the Great Composers.* New York, 1970.

Stockklausner, August, editor. *In Salzburg geboren.* Salzburg, 1973.

Strobel, Philip A. *The Salzburgers and their Descendents.* Athens (Georgia), 1953.

Stuppäck, Valerie. *So sag ich's meiner Tochter: Österreichisches Kochbuch.* Salzburg, 1976.

Thür, Hans. *Salzburg et son Festival.* Paris, 1961.

Trapp, Maria von. *Maria.* Carol Stream (Illinois), 1972.

Trapp, Maria. *The Story of the Trapp Family Singers.* Philadelphia, 1949.

Ungard, Frederick, editor. *A Handbook of Austrian Literature.* New York, 1973.

Università degli Studi di Padova. *Mostra di Max Reinhardt.* Padova, 1964.

Ziegeleder, Ernst. *Official Guide to Salzburg.* Salzburg, 1968.

Zinnburg, Karl. *Salzburger Volksbräuche.* Salzburg, 1972.

Various issues of newspapers and magazines, including:
New York Times, Washington Post, International Herald Tribune, The Guardian, Salzburger Nachrichten, Stern, Time, Newsweek, National Geographic, Gourmet, and annual programs of the Salzburg Festival.

Jones George Fenwick: Professor of German and comparative literature at the University of Maryland (College Park, USA). Several terms as guest professor in European universities. Numerous publications covering the entire literature of the Middle Ages (especially Walther von der Vogelweide and Oswald von Wolkenstein) and on the Salzburg Protestants who emigrated to the USA in the 18th century. For this work especially he was awarded the Service Medal of the Republic of Austria.

Diana Burgwyn lived at Schloss Leopoldskron in Salzburg for two years; here she was an assistant director of the Salzburg Seminar in American Studies.

Currently the author resides in Philadelphia, Pennsylvania, but she claims to have left a part of her heart permanently in Salzburg.

Her first book, *The 1776 Guide for Pennsylvania*, was published in 1975 by Harper and Row, Inc., New York. In 1981 Harper published another work by her: *Marriage Without Children*. Ms. Burgwyn has written many articles on travel and culture for such publications as the *Washington Post, Travel and Leisure* and *Holiday*.

Cover Design: Oil painting by Alice Cermak
Graphic Design: Andreas Bachmayr
Photographs: Nikolaus Yassikoff, Andreas Bachmayr,
Salzburg Museum Carolino Augusteum, Salzburg
State Archives Salzburger Heimatpflege, F. Schreiber,
Mathias Michel, Franz Wasner.
Cartography: Werner Hölzl
Reproductions: Repro Studio Salzburg
Redaktion: Elizabeth Mortimer

168.—